I STAND

THE ROAD TO MANHOOD

RUFUS CHAMBERS III

I STAND
The Road to Manhood

8 Eighteen Publishing Studios

Telephone: 510.550.5956

Website: www.rufuschambersonline.com

Email: istandproject@icloud.com

Email: info@rufuschambersonline.com

FaceBook: facebook.com/RufusChambersOnline

Twitter: @rufuschambers3

ISBN 978-0615761497

Printed in the United States of America

Copyright © 2013 by Rufus Chambers III

Library of Congress Catalog Card Number: 1-884325411

Edited and Formatted by:

Fresh Reign

www.freshreign.com

ENDORSEMENTS

I Stand: The Road to Manhood is a practical playbook that equips men to identify and break through the roadblocks that have denied us of our authentic manhood. *I Stand: The Road to Manhood* is a literary movement challenging men to boldly protest that which has held us hostage to our past all the while planting a stop sign in our present and future. Through his personal journey, Rufus Chambers III enlightens us on God's standard of manhood that can only be discovered through His unfailing love. As a father of four sons, *I Stand: The Road to Manhood* greatly encourages and empowers me to deal with the issues of my past that have reproduced negative fruit, so that my children will not repeat certain parts of my history. If you are a man who is ready to pursue the life God designed for you, follow the plays in *I Stand: The Road to Manhood*, and victory will inevitably be your reward.

Anthony L. Scott
Grateful Husband & Father

A Journey of renewal...*I Stand: The Road to Manhood* is a type of "map-quest" that takes us on a Journey of healing, restoration, and empowerment toward the divine destination of true, God-centric manhood. Rufus Chambers III has written a book that will prove to transform!

Darius Wise
Executive Director of Upstream Impact

Rufus Chambers III in *I Stand: The Road to Manhood* has concisely packaged a phenomenal tool, a compass for any man (junior or senior) to navigate life and move forward to reach his God given destiny. His personal candor and transparency unveils truth and comforts other men into the realization that they are not alone. Moreover, that God is with them every single step of the way. I believe it is not only a must read for men, but for the women who love and support them.

Lillie Hudson
Medical Professional and Servant Leader

DEDICATION

This book is dedicated to two special people: My Lord and Savior Jesus Christ and my father, Rufus Chambers Jr. (1944 – 1994).

When I welcomed Jesus Christ into my heart in 2001, my life forever changed, and I am eternally grateful. His love alone has re-shaped my existence and the eternal inheritance of my offspring. His Word has challenged me in an all-inclusive way to be the man, father, and husband He has predestined me to become.

My father's legacy will continue to live on through me, my children, and the countless lives I plan to impact through the grace of God. It is with great honor and dignity that I carry his name. I will forever cherish his love, guidance, discipline, support, and teaching. The time we were together on earth has left a mark on my life that can never be erased. For that reason, I am forever grateful.

TABLE OF CONTENTS

FOREWORD

BY
Pastor David A. Burrus

In his book *In Pursuit of Purpose*, Dr. Myles Munroe, one of the great orators of our time states, "where purpose is unknown abuse is inevitable." Essentially, what he is stating is where there is no clear understanding or direction for a thing; it is subject to be misappropriated, mishandled, and abused. While this statement can speak to a myriad of items, it is undoubtedly applicable to the understanding and misunderstandings of men. There are countless mothers, sisters, daughters, and even wives on a desperate pursuit of a concrete understanding of the men they love, yet many have come up empty handed. The reality is that there are far too many men that do not have a clear understanding of their purpose and worth, and can offer no resolve for the women in search of answers. Perhaps you are reading this and you are the woman I am speaking of; or maybe you are the man that is in search of some resolve for yourself. You are in the right place, reading the right book, at the right time.

If you have ever been on a road trip for any length of time, I am certain you will agree that the two most important factors are a clear destination and clear directions. Having these in place can save you valuable time and energy on your journey. *I Stand: The Road to Manhood* is a clearly defined roadmap of success for men, and the women desperately attempting to understand them. It is this type of clear direction and destination we so desperately need. Rufus Chambers III takes a clever approach in presenting the plight of the male/man from a natural perspective, while at the same time offering spiritual solutions from a Biblical perspective. Unlike many other books written on the subject of manhood, Rufus Chambers III undergirds *I Stand: The Road to Manhood* with his own personal experiences as a boy transitioning into manhood. As this is indeed a roadmap for men, he outlines the road that brought him from searching for manhood, to discovering authentic manhood. He does a stellar job of drawing the reader into his world, and affording them the opportunity to experience growth and manhood from his perspective.

It is not often that you discover a book that is in a category all by itself, but *I Stand: The Road to Manhood* is certainly one of those books. It is warm and inviting enough to be an autobiographical tale of one boy's quest for manhood, yet it is intellectually stimulating enough to be found in the academic section of your local bookstore. It is spiritually rooted enough to entreat supernatural growth in the reader as well. It is infused with practical tools a man needs for self-discovery. *I Stand: The Road to Manhood* is a transparent book written by a transparent author who has a passion to see men living at their greatest potential. It is through that very passion that Rufus Chambers III presents practical tools for men to confront and tackle hindrances that may be standing in-between them and their destiny. This book offers female readers a deeper understanding of why the men they love may respond to life's situations the way they do.

If there was one word that could sum up *I Stand: The Road to Manhood* as a body of work, that one word would be "necessary." This book will serve as an incredible contribution to the lives of boys and men for generations to come. Praise to Rufus Chambers III for starting what is sure to be a lifelong conversation in the hearts of the men and women who read this book.

Pastor David A. Burrus
Pastor of Hope City Church (Hewitt, Texas)

FOREWORD

BY
Bishop C. Carl Smith

"If the foundation be destroyed, what shall the righteous do" (Psalm 11:3 [KJV])? God's original intent is for the man to be the foundation of the family. However, in today's society, one of the greatest attacks is on the male seed. If we are going to strengthen the foundation of our families, we must strengthen the man.

I Stand: The Road to Manhood is the road map leading men back to God's original design of authentic manhood. Within these pages, Rufus Chambers III captures the significant struggle for countless men. That struggle is the lack of fathering. Whether your father was in your home, but absent, or your time with your father was cut short through some misfortune, the emotional impact of circumstances like these, assault the essential nature of the man and ultimately the family.

Whatever your case, every boy needs a father that will help him become a man. More often than not, the absence of the father has the potential to cripple a boy's destiny. If there is no divine intervention, a boy's developmental process is delayed and he is prevented from developing into the legitimate man his wife and children need.

In the pages of this book, you will hear Rufus Chambers III's personal testimony of how he overcame the struggle of the absence of his father at the time when he needed him the most. You will also learn Biblical principles, from the Word of God, that will teach you:

- How to overcome life's challenges.
- How to become a man of character and integrity.
- How to overcome rejection.
- How to overcome excuses.
- The importance of mentoring and much more.

Whether you are struggling with the process of true manhood or not, *I Stand: The Road to Manhood* is a must read for every man. It will challenge you to become the genuine man God has called you to be for the benefit of your family and your God-given place of influence. God bless Rufus Chambers III for being transparent and making God's truth available to all its readers.

I S.T.A.N.D.,

Bishop C. Carl Smith
Senior Pastor of New Birth Church (Northern California)

INTRODUCTION

I grew up in a working class African-American neighborhood in the East Bay (San Francisco Bay Area) where people worked hard and were committed to providing a good home to raise their children. When I was around 10 years old, I used to love to spend my time playing outside with my friends. We enjoyed the thrill of riding our bikes throughout the neighborhood, playing basketball at the house on the corner that had a basketball goal, and playing strikeout against one another's garage doors. We would play for hours after school until the street lights came on which was our cue to come inside for dinner.

I can remember one afternoon when I was hanging outside with my neighborhood friends, who were a few years older than me, goofing off behind a set of trees and shrubs that were next door to my parent's home. These friends were preparing to smoke something I was unfamiliar with and they asked me if I wanted to smoke. They told me it was weed and it would make me feel good. I was not familiar with weed, so I turned down their generous offer and eventually returned home.

These friends did not have fathers in the home and they always knew how to push the limit beyond what my parents allowed. I was viewed as the good kid and the kid who stayed in line. This was mainly due to the presence of my father. My father had a firm disciplinary program he indoctrinated in me over the years that primarily consisted of putting a belt to my behind when I got out of line. His discipline was consistent and effective, so much so, when I thought about breaking the rules, I would carefully consider the probability of my father finding out and the severity of discipline I would receive.

This offer to smoke weed was no different in that I knew it was wrong, and my father's disciplinary program was lingering in the back of my mind when I received the offer. Years later, I realized I made the right decision because that encounter helped me understand that I wanted to go in a different direction than that set of friends.

After returning home from my afternoon play, I told my parents about the proposition I received. My mother was shocked, but my father was low-key about it. He already had his reservations about this set of friends, and this new incident did not surprise him one bit. He shared a few things with me I will never forget. He helped me understand that many of the boys running the street doing foolish things did not have a father at home with them. He also shared with me that I had to make the decision on the type of friends I would surround myself with. That was one of the first times my father had ever put something in the context of me coming of age and having the power to make my own decisions. As the years went by, I took his feedback to heart, and I hung with this crew a little less.

Over the years, some of the neighborhood boys got into trouble. This made me appreciate the sentiments of my father that much more. As I grew up, I began to realize the importance of a father in helping a boy mature into true manhood. It was as if the presence of a father improved the likelihood of success for boys. Even in my teenage years as I began to date, I could see the effects of an absent father in a young girl's life. I realized that having two dedicated parents in the home provided children with the love, guidance, support, protection, and discipline needed.

As I grew into a man, I would look at my life and compare it to the life of my father to see if I was measuring up. He provided a real-life blueprint for me to build upon, and showed me what manhood was all about. I would often wonder how distorted my view would be if I never had a father present. It would have been like me taking an eye exam without my prescription glasses. As much as I would try to squint and strain my eyes, I would not be able to make out the letters on the bottom two rows. Without having the proper vision or perception of manhood, how can we move towards all it has to offer us and those we cherish?

Manhood is critical not only to the men who are trying to live their lives, but also to the people who have been entrusted to them. Men play a strategic role in society. They serve as fathers, sons, husbands, grandfathers, and leaders to countless people throughout the world.

I like to view manhood from the lens of an individual family. A father and husband will directly impact the well-being of everyone in the house, bar-none. How he performs his duties will determine the amount of pressure placed on the shoulders of the wife and mother, the amount of love and self-esteem his daughter receives and develops, and the amount of teaching and discipline his sons receive. One father and husband being out of place can have a devastating effect on those who depend on him most.

King Solomon was one of the wisest men to ever walk the face of the earth. His father, King David, was a tremendous role model as a leader, son of God, husband, and father. In the 13th chapter of the book of Proverbs, King Solomon declares, *"A good man leaves an inheritance to his children's children"* (Proverbs 13:22 [KJV]). Often, this scriptural reference to inheritance is put in the context of financial wealth, however I believe it can also be seen through the lens of King Solomon showing his children the road to authentic manhood. As a father illustrates and teaches his children the true standard of manhood, the impression can last beyond the lifetime of the father and personify an inheritance. My life is living proof of this.

Young and old men alike are in desperate need of getting help to remove themselves from the mistakes of the past and pains of their childhood that have stifled their growth and pursuit of authentic manhood. Countless boys are growing up with absentee fathers; and this fact is reducing the likelihood of the success of an entire generation. There are approximately 24 million children in America growing up in fatherless homes. This equates to one out of three children not having the lasting impression of "Daddy" growing up in the house. National statistics consistently prove, children who do not have fathers in the home are more likely to live in poverty, drop out of high school, commit crimes leading to incarceration, and use drugs and alcohol. Because of the truancy of the father in the home, many of us lack the understanding of what true manhood is and are ashamed to ask for the help we need.

In the pages of this book, you will find practical tools that will assist you and others to move past roadblocks and aggressively pursue manhood. Regardless of what has happened to you in the past, God has provided you a rich resource in His written Word that can help you overcome insurmountable odds and climb to your full potential. "Potential is always present, waiting to be exposed" (Dr. Myles Munroe).

There is an entire generation waiting for us to come into our position of authenticity, authority, and honor. Therefore, I challenge every man who reads this book to **S.T.A.N.D.** and be counted, as we advance on the road to manhood.

ONE

LIKE FATHER, LIKE SON

How we learn is critical to our mental development and literary fortitude. There are various learning styles one can adopt and perfect that will last a lifetime. The two most effective learning styles are visual and practical — or what most would call observation and experience. Let us focus on learning by observation, as learning by observation is popular, especially amongst boys.

There is no comparison between the amounts of information one can learn by watching a person perform a task, versus what one can learn through oral instruction. YouTube has revolutionized the world's ability to give and receive easily accessible learning content with everything from exercise routines, to basketball skill development, and even how to tie a bow tie, which is one of my personal favorites. The visual aid, learning by observation provides, is priceless and leaves a lasting reminder on a person's memory.

For me personally, it is much easier to duplicate what I see being done versus what I am being told to do. As I reflect upon my childhood, I remember constantly watching my father. Whether I was pleased or displeased with him, I would still observe him. He was an ever-present, consistent influence in my life, and over thirty years later, I am still amazed at all I was able to glean by simply watching him. He was such a permanent fixture in my life and a solid example of strength. Watching him provided an unshakable canvas of learning for me.

One of the greatest memories I have of my father is watching him work hard to provide for our family. He was disciplined in his approach to his career and the management of our family's finances. These profoundly strong attributes have enveloped in my mind and heart memories I will never forget. As a child, I was young and immature, but still possessed the ability to attentively watch him. In watching him, I am in awe of how much I was able to learn.

I watched my father make personal sacrifices for the sake of his children. I remember at one point he was the controller of a regional grocery store chain; which from my view was a powerful position. Even with that influential job, he would ride a bike to work while his daughter drove to school and his wife drove to work. This image is seared in my mind; as learning by observation provides a three-dimensional element of knowledge. As a child, I would question, *What does this mean? Why does he do the things he does? Should I do these same things when I become a man?*

In John 5:19 (NIV), even Jesus the Christ made specific mention of learning by observation: Jesus gave them this answer, *"Truly I tell you, the Son can do nothing by Himself. He can only do what He sees His father doing."* Whatever the Father does, the Son emulates. As we delve into these "like father, like son" cycles, there are many men who have a lasting impression of what they saw during their childhood years. Some men have positive memories that have shaped their ideologies about finances, careers, families, relationships, and raising children. On the other hand, there are countless men who have negative memories, which are more like nightmares. These images from their childhoods begin to handicap and limit them in their pursuit of the "American Dream." Due to the lack of observing the right things, at best, they pursue a mediocre life. If you saw something when you were a child, and you were unable to accurately discern right from wrong, you could be left to develop a mindset based on the wrong information.

Jesus Christ had sincere love for His Father, and in view of that, He was submitted under His authority. Being submitted under the authority of His Father, He said, "*I will only do what I see My Father do.*" Jesus knew within Himself that His father was doing the right things. As a man in the earth realm, He simply wanted to duplicate what He saw His father do.

A son being able to imitate the productive behavior of his father helps him to develop confidence in himself and in his ability to produce. Developing confidence is critical to a man maturing from childhood to manhood. A son watching his father shave in the mirror is the first step of preparation in putting a razor to his own face. Every student and protégé wants to know what works and what does not.

We all buy our children toys for Christmas, and on Christmas Eve, we get up and try to build these toys for our children. We rip open the box, and there we are, left with an instruction manual. Selected manufacturers include a detailed script of instructions. These instructions enable us to construct the toy, even when we do not possess the building skills or are unfamiliar with using certain tools. If the instructions have all of the information needed, we will be successful. However, some manufacturers enclose limited instructions. In doing so, the process of building a toy becomes laborious and cumbersome. In addition, the process is extended when we are not given all of the necessary, clear instructions. The same is true in life.

A number of men have been given incomplete instruction manuals. We have tried to build our lives to the best of our ability. However, several of us are failing, because we have not been given the correct information. Unfortunately, we are not bold enough to say, "I don't have all of the correct information."

Sometimes, it is difficult for a man to admit when he needs help. Nevertheless, if you are reading this book, I believe you are saying to yourself, "I need help. I am ready to break the dysfunctional, destructive cycles I saw from my father, or from my upbringing. I am ready to get all the necessary information to move forward and build the life I always dreamed of living."

Another prime example of a son continuing the pattern of a father can be found in two of my favorite Bible characters, King David and his beloved son King Solomon. These two men had continuous cycles of "like father, like son." King David laid the blueprint, and his son, Solomon, built upon his blueprint. In essence, King David gave Solomon an instruction manual on how to become an authentic man.

King David was one of the most famous kings in the history of the Kingdom of Israel. He had a number of great triumphs. As a boy, even before he became king, he gained tremendous esteem when he killed Goliath. Most of us have heard David's slingshot story. He was also able to unify the Kingdom of Israel and the Kingdom of Judah during his reign.

Solomon, David's son, was known as one of the wealthiest and wisest kings in the history of Israel. He continued the cycle of his father. His father laid a blueprint, and Solomon built upon the blueprint. Solomon's reign was marked by the building of the first temple in the history of Jerusalem. His father, King David, always wanted to build a temple, but was unable to do so during his reign. This Israelite monarch gained his great splendor and wealth during the tenure of Solomon.

Behavioral, moral, and physical cycles create momentum for generations to follow. There was obviously some rich successful soil, or blueprint that was laid out and modeled by King David. One thing both men had, as we are talking about cycles, was a heart for God. Their heart condition was consistent. 1 Kings 2:4 (AMP) reads:

The Lord may fulfill his promise to me saying, if your sons take heed to their way to walk before Me in truth with all their heart and mind, and with all their soul, there shall not fail you to have a man on the throne of Israel.

God was showing David, if his sons' hearts remained right, as his heart was right, they would always have a man on the throne. This was simply a pure petition of a man's heart condition. He was a man of tremendous devotion to God. He loved God with his entire being. Solomon grew up watching his father's tremendous devotion to God. He observed his father as he pleaded and made petitions to God, even in times of great success and in times of great sorrow. This observation became a lasting imprint in the mind of Solomon; and like his father,

Solomon made a similar petition to God. 1 Kings 3:9 (NKJV) outlines his petition:

> *Therefore give to your servant, an understanding heart to judge your people that I may discern between good and evil, for who is able to judge this great people of yours?*

This was Solomon's devotion and petition to God. He was saying, "God, if you can do anything for me; just give me the right heart. I want to be a good king like my father. I want to add on to what he has begun. I want to build upon his legacy." He was telling God, "I observed my father and I observed how much he loved you. He was not perfect, but he did have devotion, affection, and a lot of love for you and your people." Solomon was building upon the spiritual cycle of having an intimate relationship with God because that which a man sees; he is unable to shake. What a man sees becomes a framework for his world. Even in Psalm 19:14 (NKJV), we see David's petition: *"Let the words of my mouth and the meditation of my heart be acceptable in your site, O Lord, my strength and my redeemer."*

This was a heart condition. We see two men whose hearts were bent toward God. Not perfect men, but men who did reverence and submit to God. In addition to this devotion and strong relationship with God, we saw tremendous gifts of leadership, a heart of worship, and uncommon wisdom. These cycles from one generation to the next build upon one another. They built a legacy—a cycle of good and bad.

Let us discuss some of the negative cycles we saw in both David and Solomon. In 2 Samuel 11:2 (KJV), we see King David's attraction to a woman:

Then it happened one evening that David arose from his bed and walked on the roof of the King's house. And from the roof he saw a woman bathing, and the woman was very beautiful to behold.

This woman was none other than Bathsheba. David was tempted by Bathsheba. He saw a woman that was married, but being enticed caused him to act outside of his devotion and submission to God. David eventually arranged for Bathsheba's husband to go to war in the hopes that he would be killed. Ultimately, Bathsheba's husband was killed, and the opportunity for David to take Bathsheba as his wife became a reality.

Out of that union, King Solomon was born. Even in David's indiscretion, God still had a plan. The plan was for

King Solomon to be born through this union. Even as King Solomon was birthed into the earth, he was given a blueprint by his father. With all of the gifting, all of the leadership, all of the worship, all of the wisdom, and all of the devotion, he still had an uncontrollable attraction towards women. As we all know, most men are attracted to women, but it is another thing when an attraction begins to control and entice a man to break his character, moral fabric, and belief system. That is when we get into destructive cycles.

During his reign as King, Solomon, in terms of his desire for women, did not differ from his father. He continued the cycle and built upon the blueprint his father laid out and modeled. So much so, that his desire for women superseded the desire his father had for Bathsheba. 1 Kings 11:1-3 (NKJV) reads:

> *But King Solomon loved many foreign women, as well as the daughter of Pharaoh. Women of the Moabites, Ammonites, Edomites, Zidonians, and the Hittites from the nations of whom the Lord had said to the children of Israel you should not intermarry with them, nor they with you. Surely they will turn away your hearts after their gods. Solomon clung to these in love, and he had*

seven hundred wives, princesses, and three hundred
concubines. And his wives turned away his heart.

So, we see the cycle. We see David being tempted by
Bathsheba, causing him to sin, but David was able to
recover. He was able to repent to God and ask for
forgiveness. *"...He is faithful and just to forgive us of our*
sins..." (1 John 1:9 [KJV]). David actually penned Psalm 51,
one of the most popular scriptures regarding repentance
from his transgression. The Psalm reflects David's true
remorse as he pleads with God to cleanse him, to make
him righteous, to make him holy, and to consecrate him.

However, Solomon, after observing and following his
father's blueprint of unbridled desire, was not able to
recover as women enticed him to the degree that he turned
away from God.

Looking at my life as a canvas, there were several
respectable cycles in my life. I had an awesome father. One
of the best things my father showed me was how to be
responsible. My father had a true heartfelt desire for his
children to be successful. He placed a high value on
education. He desired for his wife to have an incredibly
good and stable life. He was extremely successful in his
career, and he was extraordinarily family-oriented. All of

these things were laid out before me to witness. As a result, as I became a man, I attempted to duplicate what I observed in my father.

Even with these good cycles, as I became a man, there were some bad cycles laid out for me to contend with as well. One of the bad cycles was the inability to verbalize my feelings. I call it a quiet internal storm. You may not hear or see it, but the strength, and the power it carries is nothing to be overlooked. A man's emotions can be deep, strong, and passionate without anyone necessarily seeing or hearing them. It is a quiet internal storm. This is something my father wrestled with, and it is something I continue to wrestle.

There comes a time and a place where a man needs to verbalize his feelings, so that he does not carry burdens, grief, and pains longer than necessary. Eventually, those feelings, pains, and aches begin to chip away at him internally, thus creating the quiet internal storm.

Another cycle I contended with was being emotionally sterile. This is not uncommon with men. They can become emotionally detached—present physically, but not present emotionally. Out of touch with their feelings, they are unable to identify the feelings that are raging on the inside.

Unable to verbalize those feelings they cannot communicate them to those they love and cherish most.

Another bad cycle men tend to contend with is a relational blockage with the wife. A relational blockage looks like this: on one hand you know what the duties are as relating to being the husband, but there is a blockage in the knowledge or passion to personify the husband. Men like to play by rules. We know how to play games, and we know how to keep score. We know how to learn the rules of the game, practice the game, and become skillful at the game. However, it is another thing to throw your entire heart into the matter. It is another level to throw your entire spirit, soul, and body into the relationship with your wife. These cycles—this part of the blueprint, needs to be reevaluated.

Common bad cycles I see create numerous gaps. Gaps are the distance between the expectations, needs, and desires of women and children and what the men they love are able to actually produce. As these gaps are created, needs go unmet, and the lives of those who have been entrusted in a man's care are damaged. This often happens when men are displaced from the seat of authority. This tears the entire family apart. When Adam was displaced from his position of authority, the enemy went in for the kill. Adam was displaced from his seat of authority when the enemy was able to sneak in and entice Eve, his wife. After Eve was enticed by the enemy, Adam yielded to her and consequently, mankind was forever changed.

However, there is good news in the matter as bad cycles can be broken. The Bible says in Galatians 3:13 (KJV), *"Christ has redeemed us from the curse of the law, being made a curse for us; for it is written, cursed is everyone that hangeth on a tree."* That is the good news of the matter. Although bad cycles exist, they can be broken. The victory of Jesus Christ empowers us to live a free life. It empowers us to not be held captive by the bad cycles of our yesterday. When we receive Jesus Christ as Lord and Savior, we receive victory, liberty, and freedom. It allows us to be connected to a new blood line, a new opportunity to make the right decisions, a new vision, and a new perspective on manhood, fatherhood, and what being a husband is about. If you have never received Jesus Christ as your personal Lord and Savior, I invite you to do so now by reciting the following simple prayer:

Father God, I acknowledge that I am a sinner. I ask You to forgive me of my sins. I thank You that You are faithful and just to forgive me and cleanse me of all unrighteousness. I believe in my heart and confess with my mouth that You, Lord God, raised Jesus from the dead just for me. I also believe in my heart that You, Lord Jesus, died on the cross just for me. I ask You right now, Lord Jesus, to come into my heart and be the Lord of my life. I receive my salvation right now, in the name of Jesus. Amen. (Reference scriptures: Roman 10:9-10, 1 John 1:9, John 3:16, and Romans 3:23)

If you prayed that simple prayer for the first time, I would like to be the first person to congratulate you on your decision. Making Jesus Christ my personal Lord and Savior was one of the best decisions of my life, and I believe it will be for you also. I encourage you to find a strong Bible teaching church in your region, so you can grow in your faith and be developed into the person God has predestined you to be.

There are some practical steps to breaking bad cycles I would like to share with you.

1. **Employ God's liberty.** John 8:32 (NKJV) says, *"And you shall know the truth and the truth shall make you free."* As we come into the Kingdom of

God, there is a truth that is made available to us. Once we begin to embrace this truth, we can begin to experience a new-found liberty because the blueprint of the past can be separated from us. We can begin to separate the good from the bad. John 8:36 (NKJV) says, *"Therefore if the Son makes you free, you shall be free indeed."* There is liberty in knowing God's truth. As soon as you have a personal revelation of His truth, liberty comes rather easily. It is one thing to memorize a scripture, but it is another thing to have a personal revelation of a scripture. *What does it mean to have a personal revelation of a scripture?* Having a personal revelation of a scripture occurs when the scripture begins to become alive in your life. You are able to not only read and recite it, but you are also able to directly apply it to an area of weakness in your life. As you apply it, you begin to see immediate change. Your past does not govern the fulfillment of your manhood. It is vital for men to receive this gift of freedom.

2. **We must forgive our fathers for the wrongs of our upbringing.** Some men grew up with terrible fathers. Other men had no father at all. But, once you come into Christ, you have a new beginning. This is what the scripture refers to as old things are passed away. So, it is critical that we are able to forgive our fathers for what they were unable to do. Forgiveness is crucial to our process into manhood. In the 18th chapter of Matthew, Jesus told a parable about an unforgiving servant. He explained that once the master found out that his servant did not forgive a debt after the master had forgiven one of his debts, the master was angry and turned his servant over to the tormentors. Harboring unforgiveness can cause spiritual, mental, and emotional torment. You must let go of the disappointment, anger, and sadness that resulted from wrongs done to you as a child. God wants you to be able to freely live, love, and enjoy life now. The choice is yours. Choose to forgive at this moment.

3. **Renew your mind.** Renew your mind in the areas where you know bad cycles exist. Ephesians 5 talks

about the husband giving himself just like Jesus Christ gave Himself to the church. It was an act of selflessness. Part of the bad cycles that many men struggle with is the mindset that husbands are to be served by their wives, and it is a one-way street. You see, that mindset—bad cycle, can become a crutch and a stumbling block in a successful marriage. That is why Ephesians 5 paints the picture of wives submitting and honoring their husbands, and husbands, in turn, loving their wives like Christ loved the church. *What do we know about Jesus Christ?* It is in His love that He gave Himself. He gave His life for those He loved. He gave His life for each and every one of us. The true role of a husband is an act of giving, not only receiving. Marriage is a mutual investment, a mutual serving of one another. However, it is imperative that we renew our minds in the areas where these unproductive cycles need to be broken.

4. **It is important that we embrace, build upon and reinforced in the generations to come every positive cycle.** Looking at my life, my father gave

me several constructive cycles. Now that I am a grown man with a wife and children, I have the opportunity to build upon that which he gave me. Part of that building process is looking for Biblical truths to add to those productive cycles I learned by observation. With that, I am not only able to have a memory of something, but I am also able to have a Living Word that completes this new cycle.

TWO

THE MANY FACES OF REJECTION

C onsider a neglected plant. It starts off as a seed planted into the earth with the potential of blossoming into a beautiful flower. The seed germinates as all its potential, possibility, and promise unite to give birth to its purpose of becoming a flower. But, this flower and seed experienced tremendous neglect. Consequently, being neglected left this flower underdeveloped and unable to blossom into the wonderful flower it was predestined to become.

Such manifestation of neglect is two-fold. First, the flower did not receive enough sunlight to grow into its natural beauty. Secondly, the flower did not receive enough water and fertilizer to sustain its growth. To make matters worse, it did not receive enough shade to protect it from the elements. This is neglect at its fullest. Because of this neglect, we have a flower that did not receive the proper, necessary nutrients and ultimately, did not grow into full maturity.

The neglect of our beautiful flower can be echoed in the lives of countless boys who eventually grow into men. This type of neglect plagued their childhood, and as a result, they did not receive what they needed to grow into full maturity to realize their full potential. Just as the wonderful flower did not receive all the proper nutrients it needed to blossom, so these sons did not receive the words of affirmation they needed in order to "be all they could be." Those words that would place light on the inside of them, encourage them to grow, and become all they can be were never spoken into their lives. This is neglect!

Just as the flower did not receive the water it needed, our sons are not receiving the nourishment needed for their proper development. With such neglect, the flower and the son can grow, but they cannot grow properly. If the absence of words of affirmation or seeds of nourishment were not enough, then the lack of fertilizer can cause problems also.

The fertilizer represents the opportunity to grow and develop through life's lessons. Fertilizer, being dark and coming from the earth, represents life circumstances that come and challenge a person. Nevertheless, in those challenges there are always opportunities for growth. Not only opportunities for growth, but there are also rich life lessons that present themselves in the midst of challenges.

However, if there are no fathers in their lives to accurately teach and guide them through these situations, life lessons and growth opportunities are, more often than not, missed and their development hindered. These boys will enter into manhood not being equipped to be men, fathers, or husbands. Neglect can start off in a seed form, but it can manifest years later into a detrimental cycle that not only affects the victim, but the people in relationship with them.

In addition to the absence of fertilizer, our flower did not receive shade. The shade represents, in the lives of our sons or boys who become men, protection. It is a means of protecting our fragile sons--their hearts, their minds, and even their bodies from the elements, just like a flower. The flower cannot stand to be in the sun all day, every day, because the heat begins to become a threat, not only to the flower's growth, but to its existence. A son, just like a flower, needs protection. He needs to be covered, so the situations and circumstances life presents to him will not have the power or the ability to eliminate the life, shorten the life, or stifle the growth.

This chapter is about rejection. Simply put, rejection is neglect. As we turn back to the Bible, we are going to look at the life of King David. The king, in all of his splendor and for the duration of his tremendous reign in the Kingdom of Israel, also suffered tremendous rejection in his childhood. However, in the midst of rejection, he was still able to become the king God pre-ordained him to be.

You may have heard the popular Bible story in which King Saul made a mistake during his reign, and the prophet Samuel grieved over the mistake for quite some time. Moreover, at that time, God commissioned Samuel to arise from his period of mourning and go to the house of Jesse, because God had ordained one of his sons to become king. As Samuel arrives, Jesse presents his seven sons before the prophet. Samuel was not sure exactly who was to be ordained king; thus, he approached each son carefully, trying to hear the voice of God, so he could ordain this chosen son as the next king. As the prophet made his way down the line, he was unable to anoint a king. *"And Samuel said to Jesse. 'Are all the young men here?'*

Then he said, "There remains yet the youngest, and there he is keeping the sheep" (I Samuel 16:11 [KJV]).

The boy tending the sheep was none other than young David. The question we must ask ourselves is why was David not presented with his brothers at the time of Samuel's arrival? It would seem as though David was being treated differently than his brothers. Why is that? Why was he in a place of isolation tending the sheep while his brothers were being positioned for promotion? This is one of the faces of rejection, and many of us have to look at ourselves and realize that rejection has been a part of our lives. Even great men have had to deal with rejection.

Rejection does not discriminate based on gender, ethnicity, or religious beliefs. World renowned men who have had substantial success in their respected genres have had to deal with the rejection of a father. Two such men include Jack Nicholson and Shaquille O'Neal. Jack is a famous American actor of Italian decent, film director, producer, and writer who has won multiple Academy Awards for his roles in such movies as, *One Flew Over the Cuckoo's Nest* and *As Good as It Gets*. Shaquille is a former NBA player who is arguably one of the best centers to ever play the game of basketball. He won multiple NBA championships with the Los Angeles Lakers and Miami

Heat. These two notable men have one thing in common as neither was raised by their biological father. Jack never knew his father and Shaquille grew up with a devoted stepfather. Rejection is an issue that is more common than you think.

As painful as rejection is, the key is how a man chooses to respond. Young David was anointed as king by the prophet Samuel. He was the chosen vessel God had ordained, and regardless of his isolation while tending the sheep, God had not forgotten about David. Nevertheless, he had to endure the rejection of his childhood before he could be positioned for promotion.

Let us look at Psalm 69:7 (NKJV). David was a tremendous worshiper. The book of Psalms captures so much of his devotion, prayer time, and intimacy with God. In verse 7, the text reads: *"Because of your sake I have borne reproach. Shame has covered my face. I have become a stranger to my brothers, and as an alien to my mother's children."*

This sentiment captures a good picture of rejection. It captures the heart of a young man who loves God. But in loving God, he still wanted the acceptance of his father and brothers. So, we must ask ourselves, why was David not included with his brothers? Why was he deemed less worthy and not acknowledged? How did that make him feel as a son? How did it make him feel as a brother? I would say it left him with a void within himself that he had to manage. Just like David, we may have to deal with the voids that are left because of rejection. Yet, this story proves that the void of rejection does not negate God's purpose and plan for your life.

What is "Rejection?" Let us look at a few simple definitions of rejection. According to the World English dictionary, rejection is defined as: *To refuse to accept or acknowledge; to throw out as useless or worthless; to rebuff*. This is exactly what can happen in our lives. At times, we are not accepted, we are not formally acknowledged, and we are cast away and labeled useless or worthless. These are what I call the faces of rejection, and as this rejection goes forward, it leaves a young man inept with the responsibility to fill in the voids in his life.

As we delve deeper into this subject, let us consider another more profound, yet intrusive, definition of rejection that will precede some Biblical insight. Rejection, in its most pervasive form, is simply *not receiving the love needed, deserved, or desired*. Rejection stemming from the absence of love can even be subtle in nature. My father was diagnosed with brain cancer during the end of my eighth grade school year and it sent our family into a deep sense of worry and fear. He underwent a number of operations and treatments over the next three and one-half years, and the side-effects were staggering. His speech and physical ability was heavily affected. The father I once knew was fighting against the ills of cancer, and I was a teenager in a fragile stage of my development.

Some of the things I used to do with my father were distant memories because of his sickness. Our days of hunting, fishing, and athletics were over. It is funny how I took those activities with him for granted when we were able to enjoy them. My father was not especially vocal about the love he had for me, but he showed me with his tireless effort. When he was unable to show me in the same manner that he was able to do in the past, a serious void developed and I began to resent my father because of his condition. I was young and immature at the time, but in my immaturity this was my response. When his love was restricted by his sickness, I responded in a juvenile manner. This was an indirect manifestation of rejection all resulting from not receiving the love needed, deserved, or desired.

What type of love is needed by a boy? First of all, a boy needs **direction**. Every boy needs direction from a father and from a mother. That direction will begin to aim the boy in the right way. Every boy needs help finding the right path, so he can grow, develop, mature, and become successful. Without this love and direction, the road can be hard and complicated, making it easy for a young man to fall off the right path or perhaps never even find the right path.

What type of love is needed? The love that is needed is **time invested**. Every boy needs to have time invested into him. He needs that time, so he can be taught, trained, loved, and corrected. Time investment is a key factor to growth and maturity. When time is not invested, we become like to the flower that has been neglected.

What other form of love is needed? Every boy needs **teaching**. It is one thing to receive an education through a school district; it is another thing for a father to teach a son how to become a man. This teaching is key, and is a huge area of neglect and rejection countless men are fighting against. They were never taught; so as they become men, they will reach a place in their lives where hopefully they will be able to identify that they do not have the knowledge needed to "be all that they can be." In this regard, teaching is crucial.

Lastly, *what additional form of love is needed by a boy?* A boy needs **correction**. Hebrews 12:6 says, *"...God chastens* *those He loves."* The act of correction is actually an act of love. Through correction, you are actually teaching a young man what he should and should not do. He is being taught how to be a son, a man, a father, and a husband.

What love is deserved by a boy? The love that is deserved by a boy is **reciprocation**. Every boy needs to be rewarded and appreciated. It is important, as through being rewarded and appreciated, their confidence will begin to develop. They will begin to develop confidence in themselves and in their ability to do the right things, and to make the right decisions. It is critical to their maturity.

What love is desired by a boy? Every boy desires **affirmation**. Every boy desires those words of encouragement. Every boy desires to be told, "I'm proud of you." The weight that is carried by those words is astounding, especially when they come from a boy's father. It is funny how a mother can run up to a son, embrace him, kiss him, and tell him, "Hey son I love you, I am so proud of you, you did a great job." However, when a father simply gives a head nod to his son which quietly says I am proud of you, that silent gesture carries an even greater degree of credence because the son has an in-depth longing to be affirmed by his father.

What happens when voids are created? What happens when a boy does not receive the love he needs, and he is rejected? Whenever a void of love exists, there is always something that will come in and try to be a substitution for the love that child actually needs. There are countless faces of rejection. As rejection takes place in boys, they respond differently and carry the burden of rejection in different ways. You take two boys who both were rejected during their childhood, and, hypothetically speaking, they can even be brothers; yet, both brothers will respond to the rejection differently.

First and foremost, a void of love can be filled with **low self-esteem**. If a boy is not affirmed, not directed, or if he is not taught or loved as a child, it becomes easy for him to develop a low self-esteem. A symptom of low self-esteem is when a person cannot identify meaningful and valuable characteristics about themselves. When a person does not value themselves, it is only natural that they will abuse their life and allow others to mistreat them. Self-esteem attracts others, while low self-esteem repels others. Receiving love makes a person feel good about their life and allows them to recognize that someone values them as a person. As a child receives love, they are positioned to develop self-esteem and join the chorus of people who love them. Parents play a pivotal role in their children developing a healthy level of self-esteem.

Another face of rejection is **inadequacy**. The boy may have to battle against feelings of inadequacy. This he may do, within himself, just like David. The questions will always linger, "Well, why wasn't I worthy enough to be loved? Why doesn't my own father have any interest in my life? Why does Mommy treat me badly because of what Daddy has not done in her life or mine?" These feelings of inadequacy can begin to grow, develop, and blossom.

A different face of rejection is **false pride**. Sometimes when men are rejected in their childhood, they can grow up with deep-rooted resentment. They can have a chip on their shoulder, and can live with a mindset of, "I'll show him what he missed out on," or "I'll show him how good I can be." This son is wrestling against the struggle of not having a father present to affirm him. It is false pride, because beneath the surface, there is a longing for a father.

The face of rejection can also emerge as **arrogance**. Similar to false pride, it is easy for a man to develop a sense of arrogance. It can become a distorted love of oneself with beliefs such as, "no one else loved or valued me, so I'm going to put myself on a pedestal and live my life as if I am the greatest gift on earth." But, in all of that, there is an obvious deception taking place because the sense of arrogance was developed out of rejection.

Two additional, more common faces of rejection are *anger* and *rage*. The resentment, the disappointment, and the heartache do not leave the boy; so he responds with anger, and sometimes rage. There is an emotional instability that may surface because of the absence of love, teaching, or correction, and the boy is left to develop by way of his own devices. His emotional intelligence can become distorted allowing anger and rage the opportunity to become permanent fixtures in the life of the boy. Oftentimes, a man cannot tell you why he is so angry. They just know it's how they respond to disappointment or to something not going their way. Anger and rage are a reality in the lives of those who have been rejected.

The final face of rejection we will discuss is **the inability to love or receive love**. As the void of love is developed, love can become like a foreign agent in a boy's life and it can prevent him from being able to give and receive love. Let us look at Mark 12:31 (AMP) which reads, *"The second is like it and is this, You shall love your neighbor as yourself. There is no commandment greater than these."*

Jesus Christ was teaching the disciples because they asked Him about the greatest commandments, and His response was about love. First, love God with your entire being. Secondly, love your neighbor as yourself. From that, we can gather that there is a tremendous importance in regards to love, and rejection is the antithesis of love. When a young man or a boy is rejected, he is disapproved and refused, but when he is loved, he is approved and accepted.

Here are a few remedies that are keys to overcoming rejection. It is important to understand, just as David was able to overcome rejection and move into the life God ordained him to have, we have the opportunity to do the same. David had a firm reliance upon God. His relationship with God played a major part in his life. Because his relationship with God was paramount, he was able to overcome some of the challenges he faced, in his childhood, and his adulthood. As we attempt to overcome rejection, it is vital that we are able to receive the promises that are laid up in the Bible from our Heavenly Father. In Jeremiah 30:17 (AMP), the text reads:

For I will restore health to you, and I will heal your wounds says the Lord, because they have called you an outcast saying, this is Zion, who no-one seeks after, and for whom no-one cares.

God is saying in this scripture, "I will heal the wounds of rejection. I will if you let Me. I will touch those voids. I will touch your heart; and I will bring healing to those areas." It is imperative for you to know that the voids that were developed in your life can be filled by God with His own love.

Here are some remedies to overcoming rejection in your life:

1. **Acknowledge and aggressively confront the issues.** The first remedy for rejection is *to acknowledge the issues and aggressively confront them.* The time of being in self-denial and immune to your feelings must come to an end. It is impossible to be delivered from something you are unable to acknowledge. To deal with rejection, we must first acknowledge that it exists. We must aggressively confront the pain of the past and aggressively confront the feelings that were left because of the neglect and rejection. As we are able to identify, then we can attempt to move forward.

2. **Receive God's love.** The second remedy for rejection is receiving God's love. Remember, God's love is the agent to fill the void that results from rejection. In Psalm 27:10 (AMP), the text reads, *"Although my father and my mother have forsaken me, yet the Lord will take me up and adopt me as his child."* That means, in spite of how you were raised, in spite of the pain of your childhood, and in spite of the flaws of your mother and father, God will not forsake you. He will receive you and give you the love only He can give. He can fill those voids. You have to remember John 3:16 (NKJV) which reads, *"For God so loved... that He gave His... son."* In loving us, He is giving us this healing, this restoration from rejection. That is the very nature of God: restoring us through His love.

3. **Forgive.** The third remedy for rejection, which is a common theme in this book, is forgiveness. It is vital to forgive the person who rejected you. As you are able to freely forgive, you liberate yourself from the control of the past disappointment, wrongdoing, and victimization. This is a

noteworthy point for us to understand, because as we do not forgive, we are giving that person or that situation the opportunity or power to control us. In not forgiving others, we are actually empowering them to exercise authority over our lives, which is just as fatal a mistake as dying without first making Jesus Christ Lord in your life. Forgiving allows us to be free and liberated to move forward.

I realize that forgiving others who have wronged you can be easier said than done. You need to realize, when you find yourself struggling to do something in your own strength or ability, you have the choice to ask God for help in the matter. What seems impossible to us, is more than possible through Him (see Luke 1:37). To ask God to help you in this area, simply recite the following prayer:

"Father, in the name of Jesus, I approach Your throne in all sincerity. I seek Your forgiveness in holding unforgiveness in my heart towards those who have wronged me in the past. You said in Your Word that You are faithful and just to forgive me of my sins and to cleanse me from all unrighteousness. I desire to live a life rooted in

love and I ask for Your help in overcoming the pains of the past. I thank You that You are a present help in times of trouble. I release all unforgiveness, bitterness, and resentment from my heart now in the name of Jesus Christ. I declare that I will walk in love, peace, harmony, and forgiveness. I thank You that You have an ear to hear my petition and that the prayers of the righteous avail much and make power available. I declare that Your power is making me free now. I thank You for Your love and being accepted in the beloved." Amen. (1 John 1:9, Psalm 46:1, James 5:16, Ephesians 1:6, Psalm 54:2)

4. **Reconcile.** Remedy number four for rejection is to be reconciled in broken relationships. If your father is still living, bring reconciliation to any ill feelings or disappointments from the past that you harbor toward him. It is vital to get in touch with your feelings, so God can begin to bring total healing and restoration to your inner being. You would be amazed at the type of liberty you will feel as you bring a sense of reconciliation to broken relationships. In 2 Corinthians 5:18 (NKJV), the text

reads, *"Now all things are of God who has reconciled us to Himself through Jesus Christ, and has given us the ministry of reconciliation."* God is giving us an agent in which we can bring healing and restoration, and that agent is reconciliation.

5. **Employ Love.** The fifth remedy for rejection is to employ love. We should be able to freely give and freely receive love. That is always a good barometer to gauge if you have overcome rejection. If you are able to pour out love upon others without demanding reciprocation, being rejected and forgiving easily, you know rejection no longer has authority over your life. I am able to distribute love, unconditionally, with no strings attached, because that is what God has commanded me to do. In Romans 13:8 (NKJV), the text reads: *"Owe no man anything except to love one another, for he who loves another has fulfilled the law."* Many times people teach that scripture in the context of not being in debt financially, but that scripture also refers to not being in debt in the area of love. We should not withhold love from people. It is crucial to overcome these cycles of rejection, so that we can be free

within ourselves and we can be free to love others unconditionally. As we distribute love to others, they can in turn go free.

THREE

THE PAST IS ALWAYS PRESENT

In the fall of 1994, I embarked upon a new journey. That journey consisted of moving from Richmond, California, to San Luis Obispo, California, to begin my undergraduate college career. This was a significant transition for me. I was so familiar with Richmond, California. Richmond was where I grew up, and up until that time, I had spent all of my life there. San Luis Obispo was a new place and a new venture for me. Richmond was my home; whereas, San Luis Obispo was a foreign place. Richmond was urban; San Luis Obispo was quiet and remote. Richmond was diverse; whereas, San Luis Obispo was not varied, nor multicultural. My new school had a mere two percent African American population and my neighborhood back home was predominantly African American. Richmond was so familiar to me, I knew where everything was. I knew where all the streets would take me. I knew all of the bus lines, and I knew all of the BART (Bay Area Rapid Transit) routes. San Luis Obispo was a new and completely unfamiliar place. Richmond was where my family was, and at that time I knew absolutely no one in San Luis Obispo.

Richmond had become the framework in my life. I had become accustomed to my past being a permanent fixture in my world, so much so, it caused me to have a distorted view of this new opportunity in San Luis Obispo. Richmond represented where I was from and San Luis Obispo represented where I was going. San Luis Obispo presented me with the rich opportunity to gain an Engineering degree and successfully position me in the marketplace. In addition, this transition opened the door for me to meet my future wife and mother of my children. My destiny was tied to San Luis Obispo, but I almost allowed my past to cause me to miss it.

Many of us view our past as a permanent fixture. We allow our past to frame our reality and govern our future. You may have been just like me. I was so in love and familiar with home, I was willing to negate and ignore the possibilities of where my future could take me. While *the past is always present,* we should never allow our past to dictate and govern the unlimited possibilities of our present or our future. In the book of 2 Corinthians 5:17 (KJV), the Apostle Paul writes: *"Therefore, if any man be in Christ, he is a new creature: Old things are passed away; behold all things are become new."* I was in a new place at a new time. A new season presented new opportunities for me. Albeit true, initially I failed to recognize the newness that was right in front of me.

Sometimes when we come into the Kingdom of God and receive salvation, we can hold on to our past and negate the new life Jesus Christ presents to us. When I accepted Jesus Christ as my Lord and Savior in 2001, the church I joined sang a lot of old traditional songs, and one of those songs was called "Great Things." In that song, there was a verse that went like this: "Looked at my hands and they looked new. I looked at my feet and they did, too. Changed my mind from the start; took all of my doubting from my heart." The song said I was new, and the scripture said I was new. However, when I received salvation, I did not feel new. The same held true when I moved to San Luis Obispo.

As we approach manhood, it is no different. This new opportunity and journey is a *process*. It is not something that is going to make you feel completely different overnight. This book contains some revelation, understanding, wisdom, and practical tips on how you can begin a new leg of your journey into manhood. Let me remind you again, this is not an instantaneous occurrence; it is a process.

In 2001, I said yes to Jesus Christ being my Lord and Savior, however becoming a new creature has been a developmental process. That is where a number of you may be today. You may be in a place where you are trying to hold on to your past experiences and at the same time, embrace a new opportunity to move forward in your pursuit of manhood. Several of us allow our past to frame our world which makes it easy to trust our experience more than believe in the fullness of our future.

Many men suffer from Post-Traumatic Stress Disorder. The first time I heard of this term was when I was studying about the Vietnam War. As I studied, I learned about how, postwar, these soldiers would recall the horrific details of the war and as a result, would begin to relive the war. Medical doctors say that Post-Traumatic Stress Disorder can occur after one has seen or experienced a traumatic event that involved the threat of injury or death. A few symptoms one may experience include reliving past events, having flashbacks, and/or nightmares. Does this sound familiar to you? For a moment, please allow me to put Post-Traumatic Stress Disorder in the context of our lives. In the past, several of us have experienced traumatic events that have become permanent fixtures in our present, and these permanent fixtures are now shaping our future. Although such may be the case, we still have an opportunity to lay aside every weight that would easily beset us. We have the opportunity to disconnect from these previous traumatic events and embrace all that God has for us. Hebrews 11:3 says, *"By faith, we understand that the worlds were framed by the word of God, so that the things which are seen were not made of things which are visible."*

God framed the world by faith and by His Word. He has presented a pattern for us to follow. If we continue to frame our worlds based on our past experience, we will never live the full life or walk into the full essence of manhood as He has predestined. This is something we must undo. We must begin to reframe our worlds with our words, with our confessions, and with the meditations of our hearts. "Our thinking must be in line with the Word of

God, because we cannot believe beyond the actual knowledge we have of the Word of God" (Kenneth Hagin Sr.).

In Romans the 12th chapter, the Apostle Paul encourages us to renew our minds daily. Renewing our minds daily requires a consistent effort and that is what is required to move beyond the post-traumatic stresses of our past. The Apostle Paul knew something about renewing his mind, as before the Lord revealed Himself to him on the road to Damascus, Paul persecuted and killed Christians. After his encounter with the Lord, he put away those things and embraced his newfound love. This required a renewed mind. I am not concerned about what happened in your past or what somebody did to you or the mistakes you have made. Those things are in the past. Today presents a rich opportunity to move beyond those past events. Men must be able to press beyond the past and what they have experienced, and get to a place to consider the possibilities of the future.

In 1994, I sat in my father's funeral. That funeral presented an interesting opportunity to me. One of my father's dear friends, Ken Tramiel, was up speaking at the podium and he was sharing words of comfort to the family, and he said something remarkable. He looked at me and said, "Rufie (my childhood nickname), the baton is passed to you." That statement rang so loud within my spirit. It was like an alarm clock awakening me from a deep sleep. It helped me understand I had a choice in the matter of how I would spend the rest of my life, and how I would carry the legacy of my father.

I do not remember what the preacher preached at my father's funeral. I do not remember the clothes I wore or the clothes my mother or sister wore. I do not even remember the color of the limousine we rode in to the cemetery, but I do remember that statement. That statement was so profound because it was as if the statement snatched me out of my current state and helped me look towards the future. It was a statement that was able to give me hope, motivation, and drive to move beyond my present circumstances.

In Ecclesiastes 7:2 (NIV), King Solomon makes an interesting statement. He says: *"...For death is the destiny of everyone; the living should take this to heart."* At my father's funeral, I had a life changing experience. I took the reality of death to heart and at that point, I made up my mind. I was going to make my life matter, and I was going to improve upon the legacy my father and grandfather created. Ken's statement forced me to ponder some serious questions, and perhaps many of you as men, as fathers, and as husbands need to ask yourselves the same questions:

- What can I do with my life?
- Why on earth am I still here?
- What help do I need to move forward?
- What type of man do I want to be?
- When I am eulogized, what type of statements do I want my loved ones and my friends to say about me?
- What type of husband do I want to be?
- What type of father do I want to be?

I urge each and every man who is reading this book to ponder those questions seriously because you have a choice in the matter. You can make a new commitment and a new decision to live a life that matters. The past is always present. However, today, you can decide to move beyond the pains of your past into the newness of tomorrow, and embrace the potential you have been given. John Maxwell made an awesome statement regarding potential. He said, "Our potential is a gift that God gives to man, and what we do with our potential is our gift back to God." *What are you doing with the potential you have been given?*

S.T.A.N.D. AND TURN TOWARDS THE LIGHT

We have spent enough time, emotion, and dialogue on the problems that have contributed towards our failures. Therefore, in the remaining chapters, we will examine essential actions we can take to improve ourselves as men. The first area we will explore is the Father's Love.

The Father's love will help us realize the power of God's love enabling us to overcome any void left from the absence of our biological fathers. We will also look at our excuses and ways to eliminate them, so we can take ownership of our lives and ultimately move past the excuses of yesterday.

Finally, we will look at finding mentors that will position us to take the journey surrounded by capable people who will add value to our lives as we march towards manhood. Let us now take the opportunity to S.T.A.N.D., turn towards the light, and arise out of the darkness of our pasts.

FOUR

THE FATHER'S LOVE

As we begin our discussion on solutions for helping men advance toward manhood, it is important to take a good look at the love of *our* Father. We have spent much of our time discussing the love, or actually, the *lack* of love, countless men failed to receive from their biological fathers. It is essential for us to realize that the love of God the Father can overcome any lack or any void left from the deficiency of love encountered. As men, we must understand that our potential is not dictated by the love we did or did not receive from our biological fathers. Our true potential can be realized and manifested as we truly embrace the love of God *our* Father.

To say the least, several of us have experienced the instability of our natural father's love. Even so, if you govern your life solely on your love experience with your biological father, you will have a limited life. We have already discussed the true, critical importance of a father being present and the value they add in the lives of their children. Moreover, God the Father is calling us to have a relationship with Him. It is through this intimate relationship with Him that the voids left from our childhood can be filled with His love. His love is perfect and unconditional. It has no restrictions or confines. The love of God the Father is pure and limitless. It can overcome and destroy every limitation or barrier. God is not calling us into a repetitive, religious experience rooted in tradition, because the traditions of men can blanket and hinder us from receiving the love our souls are crying out for. His love is the only thing that can truly penetrate a person's heart and bring healing and restoration. It is through His love that all voids left from neglect and absence will begin to be filled. It is through this healing and restoration process that a man can begin to truly experience life. All of the deficiencies, and all of the insecurities, can be eliminated from a man's thinking. To be honest, for many of us men, our thinking was developed in environments that were steeped in neglect. Our thinking was developed, nurtured, and matured into many of the things we see today. It is only through the love of God the Father; those mindsets can be eliminated, brought down, and replaced with the correct thinking that is rooted in being loved and accepted, first and foremost, by God the Father.

It is necessary for us to understand the heart of the Father. God's nature is to provide for His children. Adam was given the Garden of Eden and Eve. I want to underscore given, because these things were given to Adam. He did not have to work for them or earn them, as again, they were given.

You know, even myself as a father, I take pride in being able to provide for my children. I take their needs seriously. It is my heart's desire to give them everything they need to become successful, and as I watch them grow, that is exactly what they expect of me. They look at me as their father; their father of provision, resources and love.

This is why it is vital for fathers to come to a place of restoration. There are millions of children in the United States and throughout the world who are anxiously waiting to receive the love of their biological fathers; a love that is rooted in the love of God the Father. My children have a confidence in this love; so much so, that they are never ashamed or embarrassed to ask me for what they want. Every day, we have quite a few conversations, and they freely share with me what they want and what will make them happy. As I have grown in the Lord, I have come to understand, how they relate to me as their father will heavily influence how they relate to God the Father.

Let us look at Ephesians 1:5, 6 (NLT):

God decided in advance to adopt us into His own family by bringing us to Himself through Jesus Christ. This is what He wanted to do, and it gave Him great pleasure.

So we praise God for the glorious grace He has poured out on us who belong to His dear Son.

The King James Version reads a little differently: *"He hath made us accepted in the beloved."* This demonstrates the pure essence of the love of God the Father. He loves us so much that He wants to receive us as His children, as His sons, and as His daughters. He wants to be reunited with us through Jesus Christ. In the book of John the 10th chapter, Jesus says, *"I am the door: by Me if any man enters in, he shall be saved, and shall go in and out, and find pasture"* (John 10:9 [KJV]).

This is how we gain access to God the Father, His unconditional love for us, and His acceptance of us. He adopts us into His own family through Jesus Christ. That is the true essence of the love of God the Father. The Father takes pleasure in expressing His love toward us. His love is perfect, limitless, and is not bound to a personality, a person's feelings, or a person's attitude.

God's love is always there. However, there are times when we are not in a position to receive His love. It is as if a person wants to present you with a gift, but you do not receive the gift. The person has shopped all day; they have taken time to prepare the gift, to wrap the gift, and to present it to you. But, for whatever reason, you refuse or fail to receive it. This is what happens to a great deal of men. Due to the pain and scars of the past, they close themselves off to people, their own feelings, and even to God. They are afraid to make themselves completely vulnerable; even to God the Father. Yet, God the Father continues to extend Himself with outstretched hands. He will receive anyone who comes to Him through Jesus Christ. However, as we close ourselves and our hearts off to God, it is impossible to truly receive the full manifestation of His love.

We must also realize and remain aware of the various ways we receive God's love. God can send His love to us through a person, a song, a movie, or a greeting card. The Word of God says, *"Every good gift and every perfect gift is*

from above, and cometh down from the Father of lights..."
(James 1:17a [KJV]).

For example, I was a teenager when my father passed away and with his passing, I obviously lost a role model who was a tremendous source of love, guidance, protection, and teaching. As I reflect on that time now, I can see how God, in His love for me, sent His love through other people. During that time, there were a number of men who came into my life who added value. They provided love, guidance, mentoring, and spiritual counsel. It is clear to me that God was sending His love to me through these men who affected my life. These men were being used by God to give me the love I needed to help direct me toward my God-given destiny.

Please allow me the opportunity to name these men. The first man that comes to mind was Dr. Guillory. Dr. Guillory was my psychologist who came into my life during the time of transition when my father was terminally ill and slowly passing away. Dr. Guillory helped me process and express my feelings. He also helped me put my life and my father's illness and passing into perspective. The time I spent with Dr. Guillory was a time of reference, because I was at an extremely fragile and vulnerable place in my life. I was lost and hurting, and God used Dr. Guillory to send His love to me.

In addition to Dr. Guillory, there was Mr. Livingston who came into my life when I was a senior in high school. Mr. Livingston and I had a great adoration of cars, specifically, old muscle cars. He was a successful attorney, and had a few *beautiful,* muscle cars. As we developed a friendship, he was incredibly welcoming. He welcomed me into his home, his garage, and basically into his entire life. We would talk about cars, family, and the future. It was a bond that developed in my life at a time when I truly needed it. In hindsight, I see that God was sending His Fatherly love and compassion through Mr. Livingston.

After that, there came my wife's father, Jerry Windom. I met him over 16 years ago when my wife and I began to date. My relationship with him developed in its own timing. Her father is a devoted man who, along with his wife, raised his children in a stable, affluent home. He is a strong man who has been a consistent presence in my life. He has always been there to provide wisdom, insight, and counsel. Throughout my adult years, God used my wife's father to provide love, His love, a father's love.

In addition to my father-in-law, there was another man, Kenneth Lewis, whom God used to demonstrate His love for me. Kenneth came into my life approximately 10 years ago. I met Kenneth through church and a strong relationship developed over time. Mr. Lewis challenged me and provided motivation and tremendous encouragement to pursue all that life had for me. Not only did he challenge me, but he challenged my wife as well. This man came into my life, and God used him to position me to pursue life, to pursue God, and to pursue God's destination for me — authentic manhood.

Eventually, I met my pastor, Bishop Carl Smith. A relationship developed with tremendous spiritual counsel, Biblical instruction, and impartation. The most significant impact Bishop Smith has made on my life and the life of my family is leading me in developing an intimate relationship with God the Father, God the Son, and God the Holy Spirit. For the past nine years, he has taught me not only the Word of God, but how to intimately commune with God, Himself. Once again, in order to express and provide His Fatherly love, God used a man; a man of maturity here on Earth. Being aware of, and having an understanding that God demonstrates His love for us through others, has enabled me to readily receive the love God has shown me throughout these relationships.

It is crucial for men to partner with other men of maturity to get to their destination and mature into the man God has predestined. The love I received from these men has helped me advance in my quest towards manhood. Each minute and hour spent with them has left a mark on my life and provided me with wisdom I have been able to incorporate into my personal life. Love is truly an agent of change.

In 1 Corinthians 13:4-8, the writer expresses the characteristics of a father's love. God is love, and in His love, He illustrates the true spirit of love. Despite that, we continually, try to relate to love through our own understanding, actions, or feelings. But, to truly understand the essence of love, we need to examine the scripture. Scripture helps us understand loves intent, manifestation, and the way it is comprised.

A few characteristics found in this passage say:

love suffers long, it is kind, it doesn't envy, it is not proud, it is not rude, it is not selfish, it doesn't have a hot temper, it is not evil, it favors truth over evil, it is strong, it believes, it hopes, it endures, and it never fails.

This is the Father's love. God the Father's love does not end, and it does not fail; it endures all things. Men need to understand this kind of love. Regardless of how you were treated by your biological father, you have the love of God, the Father. His love is unconditional, limitless, and has no boundaries. It is the total package. It is necessary for men to know they are received by God the Father. As we advance and mature in age, the lack of acceptance many of us experienced in our childhood can become a stumbling block. We must identify the need to overcome those old insecurities and those old voids, so they do not govern our present-day reality or our future existence.

We have discussed the love of the Father, but what can we do about it? Let us talk about a few ways we can employ love.

1. We must **receive** the Father's love. Earlier we talked about how many of us can have our hearts sealed and shut off to God. When we do so, it is hard to truly receive the Father's love. In order for us to receive His love, we must position ourselves in a place of vulnerability to Him. Matthew 13: 18-23 outlines the parable of the sower; and for purposes of our discussion, let us put seed in the context of love.

Hear ye therefore the parable of the sower. When any one heareth the word of the kingdom, and understandeth it not, then cometh the wicked one, and catcheth away that which was sown in his heart. This is he which received seed by the way side. But he that received the seed into stony places, the same is he that heareth the word, and anon with joy receiveth it; Yet hath he not root in himself, but dureth for a while: for when tribulation or persecution ariseth because of the word, by and by he is offended. He also that received seed among the thorns is he that heareth the word; and the care of this world, and the deceitfulness of riches, choke the word, and he becometh unfruitful. But he that received seed into the good ground is he that heareth the word, and understandeth it; which also beareth fruit, and bringeth forth, some an hundredfold, some sixty, some thirty. (Matthew 13:18-23 [KJV])

God, the Father, wants to sow seed into our hearts, and into our lives. Just like the person or the ground was labeled as "good," it was able to receive the seed to hear it, to understand it, and bring forth fruit. Our hearts have to be fertile ground, so we can receive the full splendor of God's love.

2. We need to be able to **cultivate** the Father's love. The word "cultivate" is defined as: *To promote or improve the growth of by labor and attention, to produce by culture.* Another definition reads: *To develop or improve by education or training.* So, cultivation entails something being improved, developed, and/or nurtured. As we begin to receive the love of the Father, we have to nurture it, allow it to get on the inside of us, and change us from the inside out. We must open our hearts and allow the Father's love to fill those voids and transform our thinking, so we can be more like God Himself.

Similar to any other seed sown into the ground, it must be cultivated and nurtured. Cultivation is necessary as it allows the seed to turn from a seed into a tree, a forest, or a tremendous crop. It all begins with a seed. Earlier in my life, when I began to get serious about my relationship with God, there was a season in time when God would just break me down. I was beginning to feel His love. Prior to that, I was a solemn, stone-faced, emotionally aloof, and closed off man. But God and His Fatherly love began to melt away the old man. He began to purge me through crying. Sometimes I would just sit in a service and weep, and it was through those tears, God's love was being cultivated in my life. I was beginning to feel what He wanted me to feel. Through His love, I was beginning to gain more sensitivity. Some of the old wax was being melted away. That is what needs to happen with a number of men. Many of us put up defense mechanisms to protect ourselves from things life brings to us. In protecting ourselves, we can become desensitized to our surroundings. That is why the love of the Father needs to get inside our hearts and transform us.

One of my favorite quotes from Bill Hybels, the author of *Courageous Leadership*, says, "One major facet of the beauty of the local church is its power to transform the human heart." This transformation comes through cultivation. Let us receive the Father's love and allow His love to penetrate our hearts and transform us from the inside out.

3. **Duplicating** and **distributing** the Father's love. We are back to the greatest commandment. In Matthew 22:36, they asked Jesus which is the greatest commandment. They asked, what is the most

important thing we should do? We heard the Law of Moses, and thou shalt not do this and thou shalt not do that, but what say you, Teacher? What is the greatest commandment? Jesus simply said:

Thou shalt love the Lord thy God with all your heart and with all your soul and with all your mind." This is the first and greatest commandment. And the second is this: Thou shalt love thy neighbor as thyself. On these two commandments hang all the law and the prophets.

God is saying, the foundation is love; and as we receive the Father's love, we must begin to duplicate it. Once it is nurtured and begins to take root, we have the ability to duplicate it. We have the ability to duplicate it in our wives, in our children, and in all those we come in contact. From duplication, we develop into being distribution centers of the Father's love. This is one of the primary reasons why God wants to heal us. He wants to heal the broken-hearted, so we can go from being broken-hearted, disappointed, and embittered, to being distribution centers of His very own love.

I challenge all men to allow the Father's love to enter your heart, so you can receive the love you need. In receiving His love, you will be able to duplicate it and change lives one by one.

FIVE

NO MORE EXCUSES

It would be easy to read this book and think that it is not applicable to your life. There are countless books, sermons, conferences, podcasts, YouTube clips, CD packages, and DVD series on the subject of manhood. I am certain each resource was created to assist men, and the women who love them, with acquiring the help needed to restore men to a place of authentic manhood. It would be easy for you to read this book and discount it as being for someone else's life; someone who has a different type of problem than you do, but I beg to differ. This book is directly challenging you to advance further into an authentic manhood that is worthy of being a blueprint for your children, grandchildren, and great-grandchildren to model. This is the weight of manhood. The decisions we make as men, not only affect us individually, but they affect all of those we are connected to and those who are coming behind us. Unborn children will make decisions based on the decisions we make here today.

Proverbs 13:22 (NKJV) says, *"A good man leaves an inheritance to his children's children, but the wealth of the sinner is stored up for the righteous."* The scripture tells us that regardless of how we think about it, we will leave an inheritance for our children's children. That inheritance could be good, or it could be bad. Essentially, we will leave our children an inheritance of the blessing or an inheritance of the curse. These two terms are simply defined as an empowerment to succeed, and an enablement to fail. The decisions we make today will govern the type of inheritance we leave our children.

It would be easy for us to make countless excuses regarding why we cannot change, or get our lives right as men. However, we must realize that excuses can be our worse enemy to change in progress. Again, this book is a challenge. It is a call for us, as men, to accept the challenge to transform and to sure up all the weak areas in our lives, so we can S.T.A.N.D. As we S.T.A.N.D., our wives and children will have a more secure foundation on which to stand.

A simple definition of excuse is: *To release from obligation or duty of.* It would be easy to excuse ourselves from this obligation or duty of being an authentic man. That is what excuses do. Excuses try to release us from something we are called to accomplish, or something we have the opportunity to achieve. As we make the decision to seek change for ourselves and those we cherish most, excuses will attempt to set themselves up as roadblocks. As we make up our minds to transform from the old handicapped man into the man who can become all he was created to be, excuses will begin to present themselves to entice us to remain the same. "You must decide if you are going to rob the world or bless it with the rich, valuable, potent, untapped resources locked away within you" (Dr. Myles Munroe).

Excuses stand in-between you and the goal set before you. You want to achieve the goal, but excuses can prevent you from doing so. Excuses will suggest that you simply accept your past as the blueprint and building blocks for your future; no matter how dilapidated they are. In this moment, you are being challenged to press past every excuse that has already presented itself, and every excuse that will present itself in the future.

As I prepared for this chapter, I was trying to think about the excuses I used to make or currently make on a consistent basis. I found myself struggling to find one, so I simply asked my wife. She, without hesitation said, "You have made the excuse of being too young." When she said that, it all came back to my remembrance. There was a time in my life when I used to always say I was too young, or how much better things would be when I was older. I would always say that in the context of having credibility in ministry and credibility in the marketplace. I thought when my hair was gray, then I would be in a place in which I could be respected and afforded the opportunities I saw other people who were older than me enjoy. I saw the older guys in the company cars, making large salaries, and being respected as being men of maturity and wisdom.

However, as I matured, I began to see that wisdom and maturity were not always related to a person's age. At that point, I found myself being the youngest in the room in a number of settings. I was the youngest in the room because my maturity and wisdom was not consistent with my age. As I took this before the Lord in prayer, He helped me understand that my wisdom and maturity was not set according to a chronological clock or to a date of birth. He also helped me understand how He used a number of young men who were mature and wise well beyond their age.

The first example is Jesus Christ. He entered into public ministry at the age of thirty. He taught and even rebuked religious leaders who were a lot older. He taught with such boldness, maturity, and wisdom that it was absolutely undeniable.

The same held true for King David. As a young boy, he slew Goliath. He was also anointed to be king during his younger years. In addition, Solomon, David's son who succeeded him, entered his reign as a young man as well.

As I took my excuse of being too young to the Lord in prayer, and as I referenced the Bible, my excuse was taken away. Now, I am challenging you to do the same. As excuses present themselves, take them to the Word of God and into your prayer time with the Lord. This will allow you to press past every excuse that will attempt to present itself.

How do I identify the excuses presenting themselves? When the excuse presents itself, it will look for an alternate route to authentic manhood. It will encourage you to simply remain on the same path of destruction. It is easy to stay linked to old excuses because they are seared into our old mindset. However, in order to move beyond the past, you literally have to disconnect from the old excuses. Let us take a look at a number of excuses you may struggle with even now.

EXCUSE #1

I did not have a father in my house growing up. That may be true; however, that excuse does not have to be the end of the story. Psalm 68:5 says, *"A father to the fatherless, a defender of widows, is God in His holy habitation."* In this scripture, we see God and His love for us standing in the gap and filling in a void that is present. The psalmist beautifully pens God is a Father to the fatherless. He is also a defender of widows. So, you cannot look at not having a father in your house while growing up as being the end of your story.

God is our Father, and our relationship with Him is crucial. As we continue to cherish our relationship with Him, He is able to father us. Christianity is about relationship, not about being traditional and repetitive in our religious ceremonies. As we grow in our relationship with Him, He can do an awesome job of fathering us.

In addition to Him fathering us, we can also identify men who can add tangible value into our lives. These men can serve as role models. A role model is a person who you recognize as being successful in the areas you desire to develop. Consequently, you are able to model their behavior and decisions for maximum results in your own life. For example, you may model the way they treat their wives, their children, and their career.

Furthermore, mentors can be added to your life. A mentor is someone who allows you to tour their life to acquire wisdom and vision for your personal journey. Mentors can impart things into your life that will help you become successful.

Teachers are there and can instruct you in certain things. That instruction becomes knowledge you can gain and apply to your life.

In addition, advisors can be added to your life. Advisors give advice in different disciplines. You may have a Biblical advisor, a marketplace advisor, a financial advisor, etc. These are people who can come alongside you and provide assistance as you pursue your goals and quest for authentic manhood.

EXCUSE #2

My father never taught or showed me how to be a man. The good thing about this excuse is; you are now at a place where you are gaining the information you need to succeed. The Bible provides a blueprint for manhood. You are at an age of accountability, and being at an age of accountability, you can make the right decisions. You can choose to apply the knowledge you are now gaining in your life. Our lives are nothing more than the sum total of the decisions we make. With this new knowledge and information, you have the power to make the right decisions that will bring about the tangible change in your life you desire. You now have direct access to the knowledge you desperately need.

Excuse #3

I cannot let go of the pain of my past, because you just don't know what I've been through. This is always very sensitive, because again, the pains of our past are not easy to let go. The pains of the past can feel as though what you experienced happened yesterday. It could have been 10 years, 20 years, or even 30 years ago, but the pain we feel can bring the past into perfect sight. This may be true; however, if you desire to move past this excuse, I challenge you to change your vision. Focusing on the past is similar to driving on a highway and choosing to use your rearview mirror exclusively, when you could choose to use your big windshield. The windshield symbolizes the view of your future, and the little rearview mirror represents your outlook as you view life through your past. Therefore, I encourage you to change your vision. Stop looking through your rearview mirror, and look at the unlimited prospects in front of you. You have so much life to live. As you change your vision; you change your perspective. As you change your perspective; you can change the outcomes in your life. The past should not have lordship over your life. Jesus Christ said, "...I have come so that you may have life and life in abundance" (John 10:10 [Holman Christian Standard Bible]) Life in abundance is there for you. You simply have to focus on the future, and refuse to focus on the past.

EXCUSE #4

The expectations and demands on a man are just too much. I hear you on that one. As I mature and understand all that is expected of me as a husband and as a father, it seems as though these demands continue to grow. However, the good news is, you can start exactly where you are. I am sure a number of you are football fans. In football, you snap the ball from the line of scrimmage, and the goal is to advance the ball one yard at a time. If you put ten yards together, you get a first down, and as you continue to march down the field, your goal is to get into the end zone. The expectations and demands placed on a man are no different. You simply advance towards these expectations, one yard at a time. Every expectation and demand is simply an individual opportunity for improvement.

Perhaps you have an issue with anger. Resolving anger issues can be the first down you march towards, one yard at a time. You may have an anger problem and you express your anger towards your wife, your children and even at work, which can become a huge obstacle to keeping a job. In order to overcome your anger, you have to tackle that issue head-on. You can begin by trying to identify where the anger originated. Was it something that happened in your past? Was it something that happened in your childhood? Get to the root of the matter and expel it from your psyche so you will no longer respond in a way that can prevent you from advancing towards the end zone.

EXCUSE #5

God made me the way I am, and He loves me the way I am. He does love you exactly the way you are. That is the thing I love about God. He loves you enough to accept you the way you are, but He also loves you enough not to leave you the way you are. You have to understand, He is not done with you yet. God sees the end from the beginning. He has already seen you in your fullest potential, and it is His desire that you fulfill it and become the man you were destined to be. You still have more life to live. You still have more yards to complete, and I challenge you to continue on your journey.

EXCUSE #6

It doesn't take all that. Not only will this be an excuse for you, but it will also become an excuse from some people close to you. I remember when I began to take my relationship with God seriously. I became aggressive about reading books, attending services, prayer, and purchasing sermons on CD and DVD. I was in a place where I knew it was time for me to change, so I also changed my collection of music. Yes, it took all that! I had to make a maximum investment if I wanted a maximum return. Again, the return I desired was not only for me, but it was also for my wife, my children, and for those coming behind me.

2 Corinthians 9:6 (NKJV) says, *"But this I say: He who sows sparingly will also reap sparingly, and he who sows bountifully will also reap bountifully."* I wanted that bountiful harvest in the fruit of my life. I wanted my life to be a blessing to my family, my future grandchildren, and my future great-grandchildren. Thus, if I wanted to see an all-out return, I knew I had to make an all-out investment.

EXCUSE #7

I am afraid to change. Fear can be a real thing for all people. In the Bible, God was consistently telling His children *"fear not,"* even at the place of promotion. A great example of this can be found in Joshua chapter one. Moses died and Joshua was promoted as the next leader over all of the children of Israel. God had to remind him not to be afraid, to be strong, and to be courageous. In essence, you can do this thing. I am encouraging you just the same. 2 Timothy 1:7 (KJV) says, *"For God has not given us a spirit of fear, but of power, and of love, and of a sound mind."* He has given you the power to overcome your fear, but to truly overcome fear is going to require us to trust God. We must learn to trust God, regardless of what people have done to us and regardless of what people have said about us. Our trust and total reliance on God is not optional; it is required.

EXCUSE #8

I am too old to change now. It is never too late to change. It does not matter how old you are, how many books you have read, or how you were treated as a child; it is never too late to change. You know, the criminal that hung on the cross was at the doorstep of death, and decided to make a change. I believe as he hung there on the cross next to Jesus, he was convicted and realized he had made some mistakes in his life, but even in the face of death he said, "I want to change." Luke 23:42-43 says, *"Then he said to Jesus, Lord, remember me when You come into your Kingdom. Assuredly I say to you, today you will be with Me in paradise."* It is never too late to change.

EXCUSE #9

No one is here to teach me how to change. Just review Excuse #1. There are men out there who can help and add value to your life. In Ephesians 4:11-13 (NIV), the Apostle Paul writes about special gifts, and these special gifts are men and women who God has chosen to be a blessing to your life.

It says:

So Christ himself gave the apostles, the prophets, the evangelists, the pastors, and the teachers to equip His people for the works of service, so that the body of Christ may be built up until we all reach unity in faith and in knowledge of the Son of God and become mature, attaining the whole measure of the fullness of Christ.

In other words, there are some special people out there who can help you mature into manhood. There are special messengers who can be a blessing to your life and add real value to your journey towards authentic manhood. You are not out there alone. There are specific people who were birthed, matured, and groomed to help you.

EXCUSE #10

What I'm doing seems to be working for me. Says who? Ask someone whose opinion you value what they think of you and how they think you measure up to the Biblical standard of manhood? You may be shocked by what you hear. It is important that we value the opportunity to improve through personal growth for the rest of our lives. Once we settle into a familiar routine, it is easy to remove ourselves from the possibility of being open to change and simply accept our present reality as the final destination. Your past success can be the biggest enemy to your future success. It is all about accepting the challenge to advance past your contentment.

EXCUSE #11

Whenever I try to change, it never turns out right. Have you ever partnered with God wholeheartedly in bringing about change in your life? With Him, nothing is impossible. Change without Him can turn out wrong, but He said, all things are working together for your good. When you partner with God, you can have a blessed assurance that all things are cooperating to produce a successful outcome for you.

SIX

FINDING MENTORS FOR THE JOURNEY

A wise man will hear and increase learning, and a man of understanding will attain wise counsel.

The fear of the Lord is the beginning of knowledge, but fools despise wisdom and instruction. (Proverbs 1:5, 7)

In this chapter, we determine how to find mentors for the journey, and discover the important role mentors play on the road to manhood. Dr. Mike Murdock defines mentors as being *teachers of wisdom*. It sounds simple, but it is a rich definition.

As stated in the Proverb above, wisdom can be a differentiator in a person's life. In verse 5 it says, "*a wise man will hear and increase learning*," and in verse 7 it says, "*a fool despises wisdom and instruction."* The scripture here is comparing two people—one wise and one a fool. That is how we can be in our lives. There are times when people share advice, be it good or bad, and as we hear this advice, or instruction, we always have to decide if we are going to accept it or not. Some of our mistakes could have been avoided if we would have heeded the voice of wisdom.

Mentors can add value to our lives at every stage of the journey and bring us assistance as we transition though successful and challenging phases. Life challenges often present the opportunity to receive help, so we can make it through our difficulties. Mentors can provide help, literally stand in the gap, and be the difference between success and failure.

As you are reading this book, many of you are making practical decisions to bring about lasting change in your life. As you make decisions for change, it is vital to surround yourself with people who are going to celebrate those decisions. A mentor can be one of those persons. A mentor is a person who can teach you wisdom. If you are anything like me, you were not given a handbook on manhood; or a handbook to fatherhood, or a manual on being the perfect husband. Therefore, we have to seek out this wisdom. We must search for this knowledge and understanding, so we can apply it in our lives and obtain the success and the results we desire. I hope by now, while reading the book, you have made the strong decision that you want more out of your life. Mentors can help you achieve that goal.

As you search for a mentor, it is import to know the qualifications of a mentor. As we have identified the need for a mentor, we understand not everyone is qualified to serve as a mentor. In our naivety, we want to avoid choosing a mentor who is not qualified to speak into our lives, thereby avoiding the problems an uninformed decision can create.

What are the qualifications of a mentor?

1. **A person who possesses wisdom**. A mentor needs to have something they can add to your life. They need to have some experiences, struggles, pains, solutions, and wisdom that can positively impact you. They should be in a place of success or be a person who has survived a significant life challenge. A person who has overcome meaningful adversities can share their experience and encourage you not to make the same mistakes. Through our struggles and failures, we have the

opportunity to gain and possess wisdom. Most of the struggles provide priceless lessons that can benefit not only you, but others who are coming behind you. A mentor who has overcome can answer questions like *Why did you go through it? How did you position yourself to ensure you would not encounter and go through the same challenges again?* Receiving wisdom involves understanding the experiences of others and capturing everything their experience has to offer.

2. **A person who is willing to share their experience.** This may sound like a given, but some people who possess wisdom are unwilling to share it with others. They would prefer to hoard it and make the person who wants it, earn it through some laborious process. That can be a little difficult when you need help. When you are in a place of need, and you are tired of being sick and tired, you do not necessarily want to have to jump through unnecessary hoops to obtain support. Therefore, as you are looking for a mentor, you need to find someone who is willing and able to share their experience, someone who is easy to talk to,

someone who knows how to listen, and someone who is willing to be transparent and available to provide the support you need.

In my experience as a mentor and being mentored by others, I have come to understand the *mentor/mentee* relationship. Based on the type of struggles you experience, you will need different things at different times from a mentor. If the person you are considering as your mentor is only available once a month and you need to speak with somebody twice a week, that individual may not be ideal. You may want to reconsider having this person serve as your mentor as they may not meet your needs and perhaps will not provide the necessary assistance needed for your success. A person's willingness and availability are strategic essentials to use as a guide when choosing a mentor.

3. **A person who enjoys helping others.** Similar to qualification number two, you need a person who actually enjoys serving other people and enjoys adding value to the lives of others. While you are being fulfilled being mentored, they are being

fulfilled by mentoring and serving. That is how you can get into a "win-win" relationship. They will look forward to being a blessing to your life, and you will look forward to them being a blessing to your life. That is a mutually beneficial relationship. This occurs when both the mentee and mentor place value on the relationship and expect it to produce fruit in the life of both parties. Your mentor is a person who should root for you, pray for you, and speak life into you.

4. **A person who has achieved measurable success in a relevant area.** When I say in a relevant area, I mean their success has been in an area you are actually seeking help. It could be related to marriage, being a father, or just being a man. You need to see some measure of success in their lives. If you cannot identify an area of success in their life, you need to think twice about them serving as your mentor. Some people may appear to have wisdom. However, if they have failed to apply wisdom in their own lives, something may be a little off. You need to be careful, because you invite mentors into the intimacies of your life. It is great

you have identified your need for help, but you need to be careful and make sure the person you chose as your mentor is qualified to speak into your life. In order for the relationship to work, you must be able to be transparent and the person must be qualified (measurably successful) to have access to the intimate areas of your life. A mentor needs to be trusted to keep your conversations confidential and be able to provide the wisdom needed to help you. Not everyone who appears to be successful is able to measure up to the qualifications of a true mentor. You need to feel comfortable enough to let your guard down so you can receive the benefits of the *mentor/mentee* relationship.

5. **A person who can hold you accountable.** Accountability is critical in a *mentor/mentee* relationship. As you identify and share your short-term and long-term goals, you will need a mentor who will hold you accountable and keep you on task at all times. As the mentoring relationship develops, you empower and give your mentor the liberty to question and challenge you. If you believe you are going to have a problem with the

individual challenging you, then either that person is not the right person, or you may not be ready. But, I believe you are ready! If you are reading the words on this page, you are prepared for change, and having a person hold you accountable would prove beneficial. It is one thing to identify your need for help, and yet, it is another thing to go get the assistance you need. The final piece would be to allow a mentor to hold you accountable and provide you with the support you need to reach your goals.

Now that we have discussed the qualifications of a mentor, let us take a look at what a mentor is, and what a mentor is not. I have seen people enter into mentoring relationships and the mentor and mentee have a different set of expectations. Thus, I would like to share a few tips that will prevent this from happening with you and your mentor. First of all, let us define what a mentor is and various items a mentor can bring to the table.

A mentor is:

1. **A mentor is a resource to help you along the journey**. A mentor can come into your life and

walk with you from one destination to another. They can be a tremendous resource; a corner person. You are out there fighting the battle, walking by faith, not by sight, and in-between rounds you need somebody who can speak life into you, provide wisdom, and offer insight on what you are going through. Be aware of the fact that different mentors serve in different capacities. Regardless of the variations that may exist, mentors are valuable resources that bring valuable information, experience. and wisdom to your life.

2. **A mentor is a listening ear and a voice of wisdom and reason.** A mentor has to be able to listen to you. A mentor is someone who will know when and how to listen and respond. As you are sharing your feelings, a mentor is able to share timely, sound wisdom and reason based on the things you communicate. As you are reading this book, you are being provided with a Biblical perspective on manhood. I am thoroughly convinced the Bible provides the only legitimate blueprint for manhood and if you want to discover your potential, then you must maintain your pursuit of Biblical truth.

As you continue to walk through this journey, you will need mentors who have a strong Christian faith. If your belief system is based on the Bible, you would not want a mentor that would be in disagreement with the fabric of your belief system. That will only generate confusion. As you are looking for a voice of wisdom and reason, be sure to assess their spirituality. You need to check out their lifestyle, because the greatest source of wisdom is God Himself. Like we read in Proverbs: *"The fear of the Lord is the beginning of knowledge."* God is the source of wisdom. If you are anything like me, some of the challenges we are attempting to overcome will require divine intervention. Psychology may not do it because the resources man brings to the table are limited, but God's resources are absolutely unlimited. I would prefer to be connected with a God who has unlimited resources, so I can get the maximum results attainable. A mentor who is spiritually mature will be a resource to bridge the gap between where you are and the Biblical truth you desperately need.

3. **A mentor is a source of motivation and encouragement.** A mentor should be able to motivate you to push past where you are and get you to the place you want to be; the place of your destiny. We all know life happens, and there will be different roadblocks that will stand in-between where you are and where you want to be. During these tough times, a mentor should be able to motivate and encourage you. There may be days when you get up and it feels like you are having one failure after another. You may come into a session with your mentor, and you need to be lifted up. It is similar to going to the corner after one tough round of boxing, and you need your corner man to motivate and encourage you to go back out there, put your hands up, and fight your fight. You need to also understand we are not fighting against flesh and blood, but we are fighting a fight of faith. You must have the faith to believe you can become all you were predestined to be.

A mentor is not:

1. **A mentor is not your best friend.** Your mentor is there primarily to share wisdom. They are not there to become your best friend or buddy, as friendship

can interfere with the mentoring process. There will be times when your mentor will have to hold you accountable and bring correction to you. They will need to feel free enough to do that without having to worry about leaving the table wondering if your friendship can handle that type of conversation. They are not there to speak with you every day of the week, as the relationship can become common and can quite possibly become a hindrance to the *mentor/mentee* process.

2. **A mentor is not your psychologist**. They are not there to focus all of their time on old emotional baggage. They are there to push you, to hold you accountable, and to help you get to a specific destination. In some of your conversations with your mentor, you are going to talk about challenges. However, in order to maximize the time you spend with your mentor, be careful not to turn those sessions into therapy sessions. Doing so would not be the best usage of each other's time. You can get a good Christian therapist, Biblical advisor or counselor who can help you with those specific needs. Besides, your mentor may not be knowledgeable or adept in addressing those types

of issues. Mentors are actually there to speak and share their wisdom and experiences.

3. **A mentor is not a crutch.** They are not there to be a crutch or an excuse for you not advancing into your destiny. This is all about manhood. You need to take complete ownership of the process. Do not look to your mentor to drive the process because this is your life; not theirs. Many people use the inadequacies or unmet expectations of their mentors as an excuse for their failures. They will say things like, "my mentor didn't do this, or my pastor didn't do that." But you know what? At the end of the day, you have to take 100 percent accountability for where you are and where you are going.

4. **A mentor is not Superman**. A mentor is not perfect. They have challenges just like you. Even in their brokenness and their frailties, they still have valuable wisdom to share with you. They have endured and survived things that can benefit you. They are not perfect; they are not without fault. For that reason, as you begin to see some of the

imperfections in your mentor, it is not necessarily a reason for you to scrap the relationship.

1 Thessalonians 2:7, 8 (NKJV) says:

But we were gentle among you, just as a nursing mother cherishes her own children. So affectionately longing for you, we were well pleased to impart to you not only the Gospel of God, but also our lives, because you had become dear to us.

This scripture passage paints a picture of the mentoring process: the person who was the source of the wisdom imparted into a recipient. They had a compassion for the recipient. They not only shared what the Gospel said, but they also shared their lives. This is a clear example of how wisdom that is imparted should flow. You have the Bible and you also have the deliverer's personal life. That is what the *mentor/mentee* process is all about. It is about sharing wisdom, life lessons, and Biblical principles. When you, as a mentee, decide to apply these three components to your life, you will obtain the results you need and acquire authentic manhood.

The lives of the Apostle Paul and Timothy provide a great Biblical example of a *mentor/mentee* relationship as

Paul had a true affection and fondness for Timothy. He was constantly speaking into Timothy's life, as he identified the gift and the potential that was on his life. 1 Timothy 1:2 in the New Living Translation says, *"I'm writing to Timothy my true son in the faith, may God the Father and Christ Jesus our Lord give you Grace, mercy, and peace."* Here we see how Paul was writing to Timothy. We also see the level of the relationship. We see the fondness, affection, and compassion. That was a true *mentor/mentee* relationship. As Paul wrote to Timothy, Timothy not only listened, but he also applied the instruction of Paul.

It is important to also understand that mentees have to know how to pursue a mentor. It is just like identifying the fact that you need the help. Once you know you need the help, you need to pursue the help because a mentor may be a little busy, or they may have a lot of other things going on. But once you take ownership of your life, you will be willing to pursue. You may not have to pursue, but you have to be willing. You have to know you need help and be willing to go after it. This pursuing process can be as simple as being in the space of the mentor. The mentor may have other things going on, but even in just shadowing a mentor, you may see how they handle themselves. You may see how they handle themselves at work, in ministry, in business, or even at home with their wives and with their children. By observation, you can glean wisdom from just being in the presence of your mentor. As you recall from chapter two of this book, learning by observation is highly effective. It is often easier to duplicate what you see others do versus what you are told to do.

Matthew 4:19, 20 (NKJV,) says, *"Then He said to them,* He being Jesus, *follow me and I will make you fishers of men. They immediately left their nets and followed Him."* Here we see Jesus serving as the mentor and the disciples serving as the mentees. They were willing to follow Jesus, and in them being willing to follow Him, they were mentored by Him. They were in His space as He prayed, and as He studied the Scriptures. As He had intimate time with God the Father and as He ministered to the sick, they observed. By being in His presence, their lives were forever changed, and they were given memories they would never forget.

There is a passage in the Bible in which Jesus cursed a fig tree one day, and the next day the tree had dried up from the roots. The disciples were astounded and asked Jesus how it happened. Jesus used the opportunity to share a profound truth regarding faith and how it operates. Jesus' mentees used private time with Him to seek out information, so they could understand the truths Jesus knew. This is the essence of a *mentor/mentee* relationship – the impartation of wisdom.

Be willing to meet the mentor on his turf, to experience what he experiencing. We have to see the value in time investment. It may not make a lot of sense to you now, but believe me; your life can change through this *mentor/mentee* process. I recall spending time with different men of maturity and just being in their presence changed my life. As I spent time with them, I would see things and overhear conversations that began to reframe my world. My world had a limited view and a partial set of experiences that were restricted to my upbringing, my age, and my education. As you step into some of the intimate spaces with these mentors, and as you begin to see their experience, your perspective changes. I can recall being mentored by a successful businessman. As I spent time with him, my ideology about where I could live, how I could travel, what type of money I could secure through my income, and how I would raise my family began to change. My life changed by simply being in the space of this mentor.

As you pursue a mentor, you have to also know how to nurture and value the relationship with a mentor. You must never let the relationship with the mentor become casual or common, because as you do so, you will receive less from the relationship. If you do not have an expectation, it will be impossible to extract wisdom from those exchanges. You have to be consistent in your approach to your mentor, and the time you are investing in the relationship. In order to get everything out of this exchange; be disciplined in your approach.

Maintain awareness of the fact that some of the wisdom these mentors are sharing with you took them a lifetime to obtain. If you can get thirty years of experience in an hour or two, that is amazing. As the mentoring relationship develops, you will be surprised at how much you can glean through listening to a person with wisdom. As you listen to them share about their successes, bad decisions, strategies and failures, your life can begin to change. A good friend of mine loves to say, "You are who you are in relationship with." Having a relationship with the right mentor will begin to leave a lasting impression on your life.

You must be motivated to pursue the promise that life, as a man, has to offer. As you receive wisdom from your mentor, you need to know how to apply it to your life

Proverbs 24:3-5 says:

Through wisdom a house is built, and by understanding it is established. By knowledge the rooms are filled with all precious and pleasant riches. A wise man is strong. Yea, yes a man of knowledge increases strength.

Through wisdom you can rebuild a strong foundation for your life and become an authentic man. Understanding helps build upon that foundation, and then knowledge helps you excel in your life. Once you hear wisdom from your mentor, you have the choice in truly seeking to understand it. Once you understand it, you can determine how to apply it to your life. You can ask yourself, *can I apply it now, or will I apply it in the future? If now, what steps do I need to take to apply it? What resources are needed to apply it?*

As you step away from the exchanges with your mentor, make sure you are walking away with more than just a conversation, but you are walking away with priceless nuggets you can directly apply to your life and generate tangible change. It is about changing your life for the better. It is about choosing life and rejecting death. It is a simple choice, and I believe you are willing to make the right choice.

SEVEN

PUTTING IT ALL TOGETHER

When I was a young boy, my parents always encouraged me to pick up games and activities that would stimulate my mind to learn. I grew up in the age of Atari and Nintendo, and those types of games were never impressive to my parents. They preferred me to play with LEGOs, puzzles, board games, and more traditional methods of entertainment and learning. I was not a big puzzle person. I was always attracted to the cover art of the puzzle. But, once I tore open the box and saw all the little pieces I had to construct, I was immediately turned off.

Whenever I would do a puzzle, I would initially choose a puzzle based on the cover art. If it was a car, an airplane, or a fire truck I liked, I would gravitate towards that puzzle. But, as I got older, I came to understand that the cover was only one component of picking out the right puzzle for me. As I grew and matured, I understood the number of puzzle pieces would truly determine if I would enjoy a puzzle. Putting together a puzzle that is fifty pieces is a lot different than putting together a puzzle that contains five hundred pieces. One can be completed in a matter of minutes whereas the other requires strategy, endurance, patience, and focus.

The road to manhood is no different. The road will require you to have strategy, endurance, patience, and focus. This will ensure that you make it to the destination of authentic manhood. What we have done in this book so far, is lay out before you a number of pieces, which are tools to help you understand your own individual road to manhood. At this time, I am challenging you to begin putting the pieces together, so you can realize the manifestation of the picture and vision for your life.

The puzzle has a vision that is locked on the cover of the box, and it is that vision that is the motivation and the drive for taking the time to put together each of the individual pieces of your life. Your life holds unlimited potential. Realizing that unlimited potential requires you to retrace your steps, undo some of the past hurts and pains, and apply some of the tools we have reviewed in this book.

Jeremiah 1:5 (AMP) reads:

Before I formed you in the womb, I knew and approved of you as My chosen instrument. And before you were born I separated and set you apart consecrating you and I appointed you as a prophet to the nations.

This scripture helps us understand just like the prophet Jeremiah, God has a specific assignment for our lives. He has a detailed vision He determined before we were even conceived by our parents. He approved of us and set us apart. As we embrace His model of manhood for our lives, we will begin to enjoy the true fulfillment of life.

Although you may be experiencing a mediocre, negative, or challenging life, as you grow closer in your relationship with God, you will begin to enjoy more of life. We have to understand, man is not the manufacturer of man; God is our manufacturer. God is the One who designed us. In His authentic design for us are keys that will unlock all that life has to offer. I encourage you to put the pieces together.

Life has dealt many of us hard blows, but God is able to restore us to a place of wholeness and authenticity. The word "restore" is defined: *to complete, to make amends, to make an end, to finish, full, give again, recompense, render, make restitution, and make reward.* As you begin to put together the pieces of your life, I want you to petition God, our Father, to restore your life.

In Psalm 51:12 (AMP) it says, *"Restore unto me the joy of my salvation, and uphold me with a willing spirit."* In this Psalm, David was asking God to put him back to where he belonged. David was saying, "Father, you know, I have made a number of mistakes, and I am ready to get it right." He was taking accountability for his mistakes from the past, and in doing so, was asking God to move on his behalf and restore him to his place of honor, splendor, and authority.

God is allowing us, as men, to find our way back to the Biblical blueprint of manhood. He is restoring us to a place of honor and dignity. We must understand that restoration is a process and a journey. It is not a sprint or a one day event; it is more like a marathon.

For years, I was under the control of pornography. I was truly addicted. This addiction began in my pre-teen days and lasted well into my mid-twenties. Once I made a decision to come from under the control of pornography through God's love and power, I began the journey towards restoration in that area of my life. I was making an end of an addiction and being restored to a place of freedom I had prior to the vice of pornography being introduced into my life. I share that to encourage you. Restoration is real, and when you decide to partner with God, it can be a reality for you.

It is time for us as men to come out of the secret places of our minds, hidden desires, and past failures. The Bible says, *"...All things that are exposed are made manifest by the light of God"* (Ephesians 5:13 [NKJV]). That is truly what many of us need. We need God to shine a light and illuminate the pains of the past, so through His love, He can bring healing and restoration to those areas.

Joel 2:25 (KJV) says, *"And I will restore to you the years that the locust have eaten, the cankerworm, and the caterpillar, and the palmerworm, My great army which I sent among you."* This is another promise we need to apply in our lives. No matter what we have experienced, or what we have been through, God is a God of restoration. It is important to invoke the restoration process in our lives and believe it is not only a gift for King David; but it is also a gift for us. He will restore everything you have lost in your life. He will restore every year, month, day, and decade that has been lost.

Let us look at the word "authentic." Authentic is defined as, *not false, genuine, real, having the origin supported by unquestionable evidence.* God has a specific, authentic role or vision for men, and it is imperative for us to understand. As our wives, children, mothers, and fathers look at our lives, they need to see authentic manhood. They need to see unquestionable evidence in our lives that we are men. We need to produce evidence that is not dictated or governed by how tall we are, how muscular we are, or how long our beards or mustaches are. Those things are all external, superficial confirmations of manhood. The unquestionable evidence our families and the world is looking for must be found in the fruit of our lives.

The Bible says, *"You will know them by their fruits..."* (Matthew 7:16 [NKJV]). As we look at the landscape of society, it is easy to see that there are a number of counterfeit examples of manhood out there. Man, at his basic nature, is designed to lead, protect, provide, and cover his family. Counterfeits fail to do this and may be unwilling to even try. God laid out this pattern and the basic job description for a man. Unfortunately, counterfeits will fail to accept the challenge or the responsibility because their lives are characterized by negligent behavior.

There are a number of statistics in the United States and the world abroad that illustrate the depth of counterfeit manhood. Eighty-five percent of youth in prison come from a fatherless home. Seventy-five percent of teens in chemical abuse centers come from fatherless homes. Ninety percent of all runaways and homeless children are from fatherless homes. The void of a father in the home increases the probability of failure for most children. God is making a call for us to return to authentic manhood and authentic manhood requires us to raise our children.

God, in His infinite wisdom, chose the right man to serve as the earthly father for Jesus.

Matthew 1:19, 20 (NIV) reads:

Because Joseph, her husband, was a righteous man and did not want to expose her to public disgrace, he had in mind to divorce her quietly. But after he had considered this an angel of the lord appeared to him and said, Joseph, son of David, do not be afraid to take Mary home as your wife, because what is conceived in her is from the Holy Spirit.

This passage of text shows the character and nature of Joseph. Through his character, Joseph was qualified to receive the gift of Jesus the Christ, the Savior of the world. I cannot think of a greater responsibility than to have to raise the Savior of the entire world.

What Qualified Joseph?

1. **The scripture says he was a righteous man.** The scripture did not refer to his prowess, his physical features, how good he looked, or how much money he had. It talked about him being a righteous man. In being a righteous man, he was, first and foremost, sensitive to the leading of God. Joseph knew how to hear from God.

2. **Joseph was obedient to God.** When the angel spoke to him, his immediate response was to obey.

3. **Joseph understood how to cover his wife.** In the midst of shame and ridicule, he yielded to what God instructed him to do. He covered his wife.

4.   **Joseph understood how to carry God's word and God's purpose.**

Let us review three pillars of manhood. The first pillar is: you must be a man of **honor**. "Honor" means *value, highest degree of esteem and dignity*. You need to honor others, especially those you cherish and love. As you learn to honor others, you will begin to personify this principle, and people will in turn honor you. "Honor decides who desires you, accepts you and rewards you" (Dr. Mike Murdock).

It is important to place a high value on your manhood and carry it with the highest level of dignity. You need to care how you are viewed and how you are perceived. You should want to reflect the image of Biblical manhood because you know you are not only representing yourself, but you are also representing God. Sons always represent their father. I actually carry my father's name and even in the natural, I understand as I carry my father's name, whatever I do, I am representing Him even when he is not present.

The next pillar is you must be a man of **integrity**. "Integrity" simply means *you do what you say and you do what you believe*. Men of integrity allow their actions to align to what their mouth says and what we profess to believe. Talk is cheap in this era. Many people are skilled in in the art speech, persuasion, and manipulation of others by exercising control based on their words, but that is not integrity.

One thing my wife loves to say is, "we should let our lives preach." Our actions can preach better than any 40 minute sermon. It is all about having integrity. As we look at our roles as husbands, fathers, and sons, integrity is critical; especially with those in whom we are in relations. Within those dimensions, our loved ones need to be able to depend and rely on us. Our integrity is the fruit they need. Whatever we say, we need to do. Many hearts have been broken due to men making shallow promises. Those who depend on us cannot cash in on falsehood, manipulation and lies, but they can reap the benefits of true integrity. In the gospel of St. John the eighth chapter it says, *"you shall know the truth, and the truth shall set you free."*

The third pillar is to be a man of **responsibility.** Being a man of "responsibility" simply means *being dependable and reliable.* Being a man of responsibility strongly relates to being a man of integrity, because once again, we have certain responsibilities we take on, and it is important for us to live up to those responsibilities head on. If we impregnate a woman, we need to tackle the responsibility of raising the child, regardless of the relationship we have with the mother of the child.

The Bible helps us understand that sex was created for a husband and wife exclusively. Any sex outside of marriage is considered fornication, an obvious sin in the sight of God. If you engage in fornication, you have the opportunity to present your body as a living sacrifice to God and stop having sexual relations outside of the covenant of marriage. Through God's grace, He forgives us when we fall short as we ask Him to forgive us.

Even as babies are conceived within the constitution of marriage and outside of the institution of marriage, as men, we need to take on the responsibility of raising our children.

As I look back on my life and the role my father played in it, one word comes to mind: "consistency." He was consistent in his approach to being a father. Number one, he approached life with **discipline** and was consistent in doing so throughout my life. He knew how to discipline me and with that discipline, taught me how to be disciplined as an individual. He did not decide to take a month off from promoting discipline in the house; it was a lifestyle. He knew he had a responsibility for molding me into the man he believed I could become.

Number two, he was consistent in valuing **education**. Education was extremely big in our home. Education was not an option; it was a standard of living. It was really what my parents promoted from early on in my sister's and my childhood. Our parents understood that having an education would unlock life's opportunities. Therefore, my father was consistent in the manner in which he valued education.

Number three, he was consistent in being a **provider**. He was consistent in providing. He provided my whole life by working the best jobs his experience and education could afford him; even at times working a second part-time job.

Number four, my father was consistent in being a **protector**. My father was consistent in being in the house. He was consistent in his approach to being a husband and a father. In doing so, he protected our family to the best of his ability. Through consistency, he provided a covering over our family. My father was not a very spiritual man, but his consistent presence covered the family. God's intent is that husbands and fathers provide a covering for their wives and children. God has entrusted them to our care and it is our responsibility to remain in alignment, so they can receive the protection they need. As Adam stepped out of alignment and left Eve uncovered, the serpent was able to deceive Eve into disobeying God. As we are consistent influences in our wives and children's lives, they can trust, rely, and depend on us to protect them.

Number five, my father was consistent in **treasuring** his family. As I have become a father, I truly understand what it means to treasure your family, because at the end of the day, my family is what is most important to me. I have learned, possessions and jobs will come and go. Opportunities to minister and do things we love and enjoy, and even our health will come and go. But, family is something that will remain for the rest of our lives.

Joseph (the son of Jacob) is one of my favorite Biblical characters. He endured tremendous hardships, but was able to use each incident as a stepping stone towards purpose. When life threw him a crippling blow, he decided to **S.T.A.N.D.** and keep moving forward. He was his father's favorite son and this caused jealousy from his brothers who eventually sold him into slavery. The betrayal he suffered at the hands of his brothers did not put him in a place of paralysis, but instead propelled him forward. He was a man who was committed to the journey. The betrayal was painful for Joseph, but through his pain, he continued to **S.T.A.N.D.** He was able to maintain a positive attitude which enabled him to receive divine opportunities God presented to him. You must be able to keep a winning attitude no matter what hardship you face. "Our attitude can turn our problems into blessings" (John C. Maxwell).

Taking a stand postures us to advance, pursue, and occupy what is on the road to manhood. Joseph acknowledged the pain of his past when his sons were born, but he, while going through hardship, remained focused and steadfast.

I urge you to **S.T.A.N.D.** As you **S.T.A.N.D.** and face the road that leads to the fulfillment of manhood, your life will go through a tangible reformation. You will no longer be a victim of your past, but instead a victor of your promise. As you employ the principles of **S.T.A.N.D.**, your life will take on the form of the vision that burns inside of you. Your sphere of influence will grow leaps and bounds because the foundation of your life will be a safe place for those who are in relationship with you. You will go from being a person who creates problems to a person who solves problems.

S - We are men who have *strength*.

T - We are men who have *temperance* or self-control.

A - We are men that have *ability*.

N - We are men that will *never quit*.

D - We are men of *determination*.

I challenge all men to accept the call to stand. Stand not only for yourself, but stand for those you love and cherish most. I stand as a son of God. I stand as a man of honor. I stand as a man of integrity. I stand as a man of responsibility. **I S.T.A.N.D.!**

BIOGRAPHY

Rufus Chambers III is a dynamic business professional with over 15 years of industry experience who built a successful career in the construction industry. He has an expertise in construction cost controls and a teaching gift that empowers leaders and individuals to overcome challenges and achieve greatness. He has worked on numerous constructions projects in the role of an Owner's Representative, General Contractor, Construction Manager, and Construction Manager at Risk.

In addition to being a seasoned business professional, Rufus Chambers is a Senior Ministry Leader at a church in the San Francisco Bay Area. Rufus began serving in ministry over 10 years ago in a small men's Bible fellowship and has served in a number of ministry areas since, consistently making his gifts and abilities available to serve humanity. His current duties include handling the executive management function of ministry operations church-wide. He has a passion for the application of the Word of God and enjoys teaching principles that empower people to obtain their divine purpose and reach their full potential.

Rufus has a Bachelor of Science Degree in Architectural Engineering from California Polytechnic State University, San Luis Obispo and a Master of Arts degree in Management and Leadership from Liberty University. His passionate leadership, humility, and business prowess have served him well within his corporate and ministry tenures.

Rufus resides in the San Francisco Bay Area with his wife of over 10 years, and together they have two beautiful daughters.

The Chambers Family 1990 (Rufus Jr., Linda, Rufus III, Tammikka)

The Chambers Family 2011 (Winter, Rufus III, Jamila, Willow)